WILD
HARVEST
WITH
NICK
NAIRN

WILD HARVEST

WITH

NICK NAIRN

NEW SCOTTISH COOKING

Edited by Jim Shields

BBC BOOKS

For Fiona

This book is published to accompany the television series entitled *Wild Harvest with Nick Nairn* which was first broadcast in January 1996. The series was produced by Ideal World Productions.
Executive Producer: Zad Rogers
Producer: Carol Haining
Director: Jim Shields

Published by BBC Books
an imprint of BBC Worldwide Publishing,
BBC Worldwide Limited, Woodlands,
80 Wood Lane, London W12 0TT

First published 1996, Reprinted 1996
© Nick Nairn 1996
The moral right of the author has been asserted

ISBN 0 563 38729 7

Designed by Barbara Mercer
Photographs by Graham Lees

Set in Spectrum, Felix and Gill Sans Condensed by Ace Filmsetting Ltd, Frome
Printed in Great Britain by Cambus Litho Ltd, East Kilbride
Bound in Great Britain by Hunter & Foulis Ltd, Edinburgh
Colour separations by Radstock Reproductions Ltd, Midsomer Norton
Jacket printed by Lawrence Allen Ltd, Weston-super-Mare

CONTENTS

ACKNOWLEDGEMENTS

I would like to thank – Ideal World Productions and BBC Scotland for giving me this opportunity; Jim Shields, Carol Haining and all the crew members who worked long and hard to make the series; Graham Lees for his beautiful photographs; Jean, Dan and all of the staff at Braeval for being the best; Suzanne Webber and Vanessa Daubney at BBC Books; thanks again to Jim Shields for his invaluable help with the book and his astonishing ability to read my writing; and finally, Mum and Dad who have always given me their unwavering support.

INTRODUCTION

Making good food to restaurant standard does not have to be complicated or involved. The most important things in any dish are the
ingredients, and the best way to plan a meal is to find the freshest and
best ingredients possible – then use a recipe which suits them. This is
how I work at my restaurant, Braeval, and it's a philosophy I have
stuck to in my ten years as a self-taught chef.

In my television programme, I had to schlep out of bed at un-
earthly hours, to experience the delights of scallop dredging or deer
stalking, in order to obtain the best raw materials for my recipes. All
you have to do, however, is cultivate a butcher and fishmonger to
ensure that you are always cooking with only the best!

Before you get into the book proper, here are a few tips to bear in
mind:

1 Please read each recipe through to the end and try and visualise all
the steps *before* you start cooking.
2 Always plan well ahead. Don't try to make stocks, for example, on
the day of a dinner party. Make them when you have the time and
freeze them until needed.
3 Write out a list of the jobs required and cross them out as you go.
A panic only happens when you leave everything to the last
minute.
4 Start with easier dishes and work up to more difficult ones.
5 Don't plan a menu with three or four difficult courses – concentrate on *one* 'involved' course and make it well, keeping the others
simple. (For example: Soup for the starter followed by a more

difficult main course and finished off with an easy pudding. In this way, the soup and the pudding can be made the previous day, leaving you to concentrate on the main course.)

Finally, I would like to thank my wife Fiona, and I'd also like to thank the following pals for their help and encouragement over the years:
Eric and Betty Allen (Airds Hotel)
David and Hilary Brown (La Potinière)
David and Pat Wilson (Peat Inn)
and Jim Kerr
That's enough philosophy and thank you's, let's hit the book . . .

Nick Nairn

SPECIAL EQUIPMENT

Here is a list of some kitchen equipment which will actively help your cooking ambitions, rather than clutter up your kitchen drawers:

FRYING PANS: The best to use are black iron. They are all metal, which means that they can be put straight into the oven. They need to be seasoned prior to use (not unlike a wok) and are superb for cooking with. Also, they're cheap and last forever.

MANDOLIN GRATER: Not essential, but very useful for larger quantities of slicing and grating. It has the added advantage of being millimetre-accurate for fine slicing.

CHINOIS SIEVE: A fine mesh metal sieve. Very handy for straining stocks and sauces.

PASTA MACHINE: Indispensable for fresh pasta.

SCONE CUTTERS: Buy the heaviest and strongest you can find. They are useful for cutting out Dauphinoise potatoes, shaping fishcakes, salmon tartares and many other things – including scones, I suppose.

HAND-HELD BLENDER: Or 'stick liquidiser'. These small electric liquidisers have revolutionised sauce making, allowing anyone to make light, frothy sauces and banishing 'split' sauces to the past.

KILNER JARS: These swing top jars with replaceable rubber seals are handy for storing Pesto, Tapenade, Home Dried Tomatoes and practically anything else you can cram them with. Give them a good old wash before use and ensure that anything kept in them is covered in olive oil.

KNIVES: A large chef's knife (I use a 30 cm/12 in knife) and a flexible boning knife combined with a good chopping board and a sharpening steel will aid your cooking no end.

Other useful implements are a quality lemon zester, a good quality canalle cutter and a stainless steel conical strainer.

Getting good quality gear means saving time and effort on the day, so it *is* worth treating yourself – even if it's in instalments.

SEASONING: A wee word on seasoning. In most of the following recipes, you'll see that Maldon salt is ubiquitous. It's not as coarse as sea salt and better by far than regular salt. (The Men from Maldon haven't given me a bung for this, by the way, it has quite simply become an essential ingredient to my cooking.) I hardly ever use black pepper, as I find the flavour very invasive, so I mainly use fresh ground white pepper.

PART ONE

SOUPS

SOUPS – AN INTRODUCTION

I love soup. I find it a very comforting thing, both to make and eat.
Especially with slices of freshly-baked bread slathered with good,
unsalted butter. My own soups seldom have stock in them, I rely on
good technique to get the best flavours from the ingredients.

BASIC SOUP RULES:

1) Use a ratio of approximately 25% onion to the main vegetable
   ingredient.
2) Cut the vegetables into the smallest pieces practicable – a 5 mm
   (¼ in) dice. This reduces cooking time. (An electric food slicer is a
   handy thing for this.)
3) Always add *boiling* water to the vegetables as this reduces the time
   that the soup is off the boil where it can 'stew' and lose its
   freshness.
4) Once cooked, liquidise the soup and cool it as quickly as possible –
   this keeps its quality and flavour.
5) It's much easier to make a big batch of soup. That way you can

freeze it in handy-size portions and then reliquidise it once defrosted and re-heated.

6) The soup is cooked once the vegetables are soft and tender. Timing varies for different vegetables.

APPROXIMATE COOKING TIME FOR VEGETABLES:

Artichoke: 35 minutes.

Broccoli: 10 minutes.

Carrot: 45 minutes.

Cauliflower: 45 minutes.

Mushroom: 40 minutes.

Parsnip: 50 minutes.

Pea: 3 minutes.

Spinach: 5 minutes.

Tomato: 20 minutes.

Watercress: 2 minutes.

All of the following soups, apart from Gazpacho, freeze very well.

CARROT, HONEY AND GINGER SOUP

Fabby colour. Easy to make. Tastes great. Cheap. What more do you want?

80 g (3 oz) unsalted butter

150 g (5 oz) onion, thinly sliced

20 g (¾ oz) root ginger, peeled

600 g (1½ lb) carrots, peeled and grated

1 tablespoon clear honey

1 teaspoon lemon juice

2 teaspoons Maldon salt

5 turns fresh ground white pepper

900 ml (1½ pints) boiling water

SERVES SIX

Melt the butter in a large saucepan. Add the onions and stir to coat — don't let the onions go brown. Using the flat edge of a heavy knife, crush the ginger (this releases the oil). Add this to the onions and let them sweat for ten minutes.

Now add the grated carrot, honey, lemon juice and seasoning. Stir well. Pour in the boiling water and bring it back to boil. Simmer for 45 minutes. (You may have to add a little more water during this time to allow for evaporation).

Remove the pan from the heat and liquidise the contents (with a hand-held blender or in the liquidiser) until smooth and creamy.

Check the seasoning and serve.

If freezing, allow it to cool before pouring it into a sealable tub and placing it into freezer. If not freezing, this soup will keep for three days in the fridge.

WILD MUSHROOM SOUP

The intense mushroom flavour and the thick, rich texture make this my all-time favourite soup. Mushrooms actually make the best soup when they're a few days old and have started to darken a bit, and I usually buy up any older (and cheaper) baskets when they're available.

The best variety of mushrooms for this soup are Paris Browns, which are fairly readily available. Ordinary button mushrooms can be used, and, if you can find them, add 15 g (½ oz) of dried ceps for extra flavour.

Melt the butter in a large saucepan and gently sweat the onions and garlic for 10 minutes until soft. Add the mushrooms (including dried ceps, if you're using them) and stir to coat. Now add the Soy and the seasoning and finally the boiling water.

Bring back to the boil, then simmer for 40 minutes until the mushrooms are tender. Liquidise the soup and check your seasoning.

If serving immediately, garnish with a squiggle of cream and some greenery (chives, flat parsley, basil or tarragon), or drop on a few sliced, sautéed mushrooms.

50 g (2 oz) unsalted butter
100 g (4 oz) onion, thinly sliced
1 clove garlic, crushed
450 g (1 lb) Paris Browns (or chestnut mushrooms)
15 g (½ oz) dried ceps (optional)
25 ml (1 fl oz) light Soy Sauce
½ teaspoon salt
5 turns fresh ground white pepper
600 ml (1 pint) boiling water

Pinch chives or flat parsley or basil or tarragon
60 ml (½ fl oz) fresh cream

SERVES SIX

LEFT: Carrot, Honey and Ginger
Soup (page 12). RIGHT: Gazpacho
(page 17).

PARSNIP AND CHILLI OIL SOUP

The chilli combines well with the flavour of the parsnips to make a warming soup, best enjoyed in winter – which just happens to be when parsnips are at their best. By the way, if the parsnips are large and 'woody', cut out the hard centre before slicing.

100 g (4 oz) unsalted butter
225 g (8 oz) onions, thinly sliced
900 g (2 lb) peeled parsnips, sliced
  across diameters
2 teaspoons Chilli Oil (see page
  169)
15 g (½ oz) Maldon salt
900 ml (1½ pints) boiling water

Olive Oil Croûtons (see page 175)
Parmesan shavings

SERVES EIGHT

Melt the butter in a large saucepan and sweat the onions for about ten minutes until they are soft. Add the parsnips, Chilli Oil and salt. Stir to coat the onions and add the boiling water. Bring back to the boil, then reduce the heat. Simmer for 50 minutes and then liquidise. Check and adjust seasoning.

If serving immediately, you can garnish it with some Olive Oil Croûtons and a few shavings of Parmesan.

Alternatively, leave the soup to cool. It keeps for six weeks in the freezer, three days in the fridge.

GAZPACHO

This Spanish speciality is a sort of half soup/half salad and is not only vegetarian, but, because of its zero saturated fat content, is also healthy to eat. It is only as good as the ingredients however, so seek out ripe, fresh plum tomatoes and nice big, juicy ripe peppers. It also benefits from being made a day in advance, which allows all the flavours to mellow. Fabulous on a hot summer day, try garnishing each serving with a frozen olive oil cube, made in your freezer ice tray.

Remove the green growing 'eyes' of the tomatoes (cutting them in half first is the easiest way), then quarter them. Quarter and de-seed the peppers, then roughly chop them into 1 cm (½ in) bits. Peel and roughly chop the onion similarly.

Peel the cucumber using a potato peeler and cut it in half lengthwise. Using a teaspoon, scoop out the seeds and discard them. Then roughly chop the flesh like the peppers and onion. Peel and crush the garlic cloves and remove any thick stems from the basil.

Dump all the ingredients into a food processor and give them a good old whizz for approximately one minute. *Don't* work it into a mush – Gazpacho should have a nice, chunky texture.

Check the seasoning, then chill the Gazpacho until needed. And that's it. It tastes best when made a day in advance and keeps for up to three days in the fridge. Sadly, it doesn't freeze very well, but on the other hand, it can also be used to great effect as a sauce for roast salmon or seabass.

Serve in a shallow bowl with a frozen olive oil cube plopped into it and a scattering of freshly chopped basil leaves.

900 g (2 lb) ripe, plum tomatoes
3 ripe, red peppers
1 large red onion
1 cucumber
2 cloves of garlic
15 g (¼ oz) fresh basil
120 ml (4 fl oz) olive oil
60 ml (2 fl oz) red wine vinegar
15 g (½ oz) Maldon salt
12 turns fresh ground black pepper

Olive oil cubes (see above)
Fresh basil, chopped

SERVES TWELVE

ARTICHOKE AND SMOKED BACON SOUP

Definitely my favourite use for Jerusalem artichokes. These are rather unassuming, knobbly roots, and a bit of a pain to peel, but they have a knockout smokey flavour that works a treat with the smoked bacon.

900 g (2 lb) Jerusalem artichokes
Squeeze of lemon juice
5 rashers smoked back bacon
2 tablespoons sunflower oil
75 g (3 oz) unsalted butter
225 g (8 oz) onions, thinly sliced
11 g (⅓ oz) Maldon salt
12 turns fresh ground white pepper
1.2 litres (2 pints) boiling water

Pinch snipped chives or chopped
  parsley

SERVES EIGHT

Peel the artichokes with a potato peeler, then place immediately into bowl of cold water with a squeeze of lemon juice (to prevent them turning brown).

Chop the bacon into matchsticks. Then heat a large pot until hot, pour in the sunflower oil, followed rapidly by the bacon. Fry until nicely crisp, stirring with a wooden spoon. Remove just under half the amount of bacon from the pan and leave aside to use as a garnish.

Add the butter and, as soon as it starts to foam, add the onions and stir until everything is well coated. Reduce the heat and sweat for ten minutes.

While you're waiting for the onions to soften, thinly slice the artichokes (a mandolin grater is perfect for this or use a box grater for a finer texture). Add them straight away to the onions and bacon, followed by the seasoning and the boiling water.

Bring back to the boil before reducing to a simmer and cook for 35 minutes until the artichoke is tender. Liquidise and check the seasoning.

Serve immediately and garnish with a few snipped chives or chopped parsley and the reserved bacon.

Alternatively, allow the soup to cool before freezing. (It keeps for six weeks frozen or three days in the fridge.)

PART TWO

FISH STARTERS

FISH – AN INTRODUCTION

Buying a ready-filleted fish is always a bit of a gamble, since you never know how fresh the thing is. Always try to get a fishmonger to fillet from a whole fish for you. It *is* his job, after all. That aside, not only is fish very good for you, it is also an exciting and rewarding raw ingredient, offering flavour and variety.

When buying fish, look out for the following:

- Bright, prominent eyes – not dull and sunken.
- Pink gills with no trace of brown.
- Should have a clear, odourless slime on skin – no dryness.
- Flesh should be firm, not flabby.
- Should have a clean, sea odour – shouldn't smell 'fishy'.
- No bruising on the flesh.

Shellfish should be bought alive. If this is not possible, look out for these tell-tale signs: fresh shellfish have a clean smell, not a strong odour. With mussels and scallops, the fresh fish have tightly closed shells.

Now let's get on with it.

Seared fillet of salmon with an avocado salsa and oriental sauce vierge

This is currently the favourite dish I serve at Braeval. It's simple, elegant and easy to do – yet it's full of sophisticated flavours and contrasts of colour and temperature.

I use farmed Shetland salmon, since its slightly higher oil content helps it withstand the fierce heat of the flash frying.

You can make the salsa and the sauce up to 12 hours ahead of time, leaving you only the final flash frying to finish.

Ask your fishmonger to cut the salmon escalopes for you.

4 × 75 g (3 oz) thin salmon
  escalopes, skinned and boned
3 tablespoons sunflower oil
Juice of ½ a lime
Maldon salt
Fresh ground white pepper

FOR THE SALSA:
1 ripe avocado
1 red chilli, de-seeded and finely
  chopped
1 teaspoon chopped, fresh coriander
  leaves
1 teaspoon finely chopped Japanese
  pickled ginger (available from
  Chinese supermarkets)
2 Tomatoes Concasse (see page 171)
1 tablespoon Thai fish sauce
Pinch of Maldon salt
Zest and juice of ½ lime

FOR THE SAUCE:
120 ml (4 fl oz) Oriental Sauce
  Vierge (see page 177)

SERVES FOUR

For the Salsa, halve the avocado and remove the stone. Halve again and remove the skin before chopping it into 10 mm (½ in) chunks.

Place in a mixing bowl and add the chilli, coriander, Japanese pickled ginger, Tomato Concasse, Nam Plas sauce, a pinch of Maldon salt and the zest and juice of half a lime. Mix well and leave at room temperature for a minimum of 30 minutes to allow the flavours to develop.

For the main dish, heat a large frying pan through to very hot. In a saucepan, warm through the Oriental Sauce Vierge. Have four warmed serving plates ready for use.

Add the sunflower oil to the hot frying pan. As soon as it smokes, add two of the escalopes and cook for approximately two minutes on one side only. Place the escalopes seared side up in a metal tray and keep them warm. Repeat with the two other fillets before seasoning all four with the juice of half a lime, crushed Maldon salt and fresh ground white pepper. Keep the escalopes warm.

Divide the Salsa into four neat piles in the centre of each serving plate. Stir the Oriental Sauce Vierge and spoon it around the Salsa. Place a salmon escalope onto each Salsa pile and serve immediately.

LASAGNE OF SEARED SALMON, SAMPHIRE AND TOMATO WITH A FROTHY HERB SAUCE

Samphire (or seagrass) is like a cross between asparagus and seaweed, and grows in marshy sea estuaries. It has a fresh, salty flavour and a vibrant green colour. It's available in early summer and although most of the samphire I use is from Normandy, there *is* some Scottish stuff from the West coast. It is available from specialist greengrocers or fishmongers. If you can't get samphire, wilted spinach leaves are a good alternative. Freshly made pasta is preferable and can be trimmed down to the correct size straight away, but the dried stuff will do and can be cut to size after the initial cooking.

Place a large pan, half filled with water, on to a simmer and heat a frying pan until hot. In a small saucepan, warm through the Nage Butter Sauce.

Adding the sunflower oil to the hot frying pan, quickly fry the salmon escalopes on one side only. When the edges are browned (approx. two minutes), remove them to a tray, seared side up. Season with salt, pepper and lemon juice, and keep warm. Add the pasta to the hot water and warm through for 90 seconds. Remove the pasta with a slotted spoon and drain it on a clean tea towel. Add the samphire to the water for 60 seconds and drain it.

On each of four warmed serving plates, place a sheet of hot lasagne. Corrugate it by placing your fingertips on opposite edges of the sheet and gently pushing together to give it some height. Scatter the samphire equally over each sheet of lasagne and sprinkle the diced tomato over this.

Add the herbs to the warm Nage Butter Sauce with the whipped cream and whizz well with a hand blender until foamy. Check the seasoning. Spoon this over the pasta, samphire and tomato and place the salmon escalopes on top. Serve pronto.

4 x 75 g (3 oz) salmon escalopes, skinned and boned

4 x 10 cm x 10 cm (4 x 4 in) sheets of lasagne, cooked as per packet instructions and cooled in cold water and drained

150 ml (5 fl oz) warmed Nage Butter Sauce (see page 164)

2 tablespoons sunflower oil

100 g (4 oz) samphire

2 plum Tomatoes Concasse (see page 171)

1 tablespoon double cream, lightly whipped

1 tablespoon chives, chopped

1 tablespoon chervil, chopped

1 tablespon dill, chopped

Maldon salt

Fresh ground white pepper

Lemon juice

SERVES FOUR

TARTARE OF SALMON WITH CUCUMBER SPAGHETTI AND OLIVE OIL SAUCE

This is a simplified version of Raymond Blanc's classic and is terrific for dinner parties. Since all the preparation for this dish is done well in advance, your guests needn't know until they've eaten it (and pronounced it delicious) that they've just consumed raw fish.

FOR THE TARTARE AND CUCUMBER SPAGHETTI:

225 g (8 oz) salmon fillet, boned and skinned

1 small cucumber (or ½ large cucumber)

2 small shallots, finely chopped

2 teaspoons chives, chopped

50 ml (2 fl oz) crème fraîche

2 small gherkins, finely diced

Maldon salt

Fresh ground white pepper

Juice of 1 lemon

1 teaspoon cooking salt

FOR THE OLIVE OIL SAUCE:

100 ml (3 fl oz) extra virgin olive oil

4 tablespoons chervil, chopped

Maldon salt

Fresh ground white pepper

1 tablespoon lemon juice

SERVES FOUR

For the Tartare, cut the salmon fillet into 5 mm (¼ in) slices, then cut again into 5 mm (¼ in) strips, finally dice into 5 mm (¼ in) cubes.

Combine the diced salmon with the shallots, chives, crème fraîche, gherkins, half of the lemon juice and season to taste. Allow to marinate for three to four hours before checking the seasoning again. Use a scone cutter 60 cm (2¼ in) in diameter as a mould to shape the salmon cubes into little cake shapes. Place them on a tray until you are ready to use them.

For the Cucumber Spaghetti, peel and cut the cucumber in half lengthwise. Remove the seeds with a teaspoon before cutting the cucumber into long, spaghetti-like strands. I use a mandolin grater for this, but it can be done with a knife by hand. Alternatively, you can just dice it – it still tastes as good! Salt the cucumber and allow it to drain in a sieve or colander for five to six minutes and then wash off the salt and allow it to drain for a further 30 minutes.

For the Olive Oil Sauce, combine the olive oil, chervil, seasoning and lemon juice in a small bowl. Taste it for seasoning!

To serve, place one of the Tartares in the centre of a plate. Pile some cucumber spaghetti on top and drizzle a little olive oil sauce around the tartare, but not over it.

For extra Brownie points when making the

Tartare, leave out the crème fraîche until after the fish has been marinated, then fill the pastry cutter only four fifths full. Fill the remaining fifth with a dollop of crème fraîche and smooth off the top with a palette knife. Remove the cutter and marvel at how impressive it looks.

SALMON AND COD FISHCAKE WITH WILTED LEAVES AND A RED PEPPER AND CORIANDER SAUCE

This dish has become a classic at Braeval, proving that food doesn't have to be 'fancy' to be good. Not only a great way of using up left over bits of fish or mashed potato, I believe fishcakes deserve the best ingredients possible. I've also found that coating them with breadcrumbs is easier to do if the patties are frozen first and, of course, cooking them from frozen makes them an ideal standby dish.

Pre-heat the oven to 230°C/450°F/Gas Mark 8.

Use half of the butter to grease a roasting tin big enough to hold the salmon and cod fillets comfortably. Dot the remaining butter over the fish in pinch-sized lumps. Pour the lemon juice over and add the salt, the pepper and Chilli Oil.

Bake the fish for approximately five minutes until just cooked, allowing the fish to still be *slightly* undercooked in the centre. Once out of the oven, allow the fish to stand for five minutes.

Put the mashed potato (this can be hot or cold) into a large mixing bowl and add the fish and spring onions. Fold together with a wooden spoon until the fish is well mixed through. Taste and adjust your seasoning if required.

Cover a household tray (tin or plastic) with greaseproof paper and using a scone cutter 6 cm (2¼ in) in diameter, shape the mix into 12 fishcakes

FOR THE FISHCAKES:

450 g (1 lb) salmon fillet, skinned and boned

450 g (1 lb) cod fillet, skinned and boned

450 g (1 lb) Mashed Potatoes (see page 127)

100 g (4 oz) unsalted butter

Juice of 1 lemon

2 teaspoons Maldon salt, crushed

12 turns fresh ground white pepper

2 teaspoons Chilli Oil (see page 169)

6 spring onions, finely chopped

200 g (8 oz) Breadcrumbs (see page 173)

4 whole eggs, size 3
200 g (8 oz) plain flour, sifted
Maldon salt and white pepper to
  season

MAKES
12–14 FISHCAKES.
THE COMPLETE RECIPE
SERVES FOUR

FOR THE COMPLETE
RECIPE:

Sunflower oil to fry
4 Fishcakes, frozen
2 handfuls salad leaves, mixed (lollo
  rosso, oakleaf, curly endive,
  radiccio, rocket, chervil)
2 teaspoons olive oil
½ teaspoon lemon juice
Pinch of Maldon salt
2 turns fresh ground white pepper
150 ml (5 fl oz) Nage Butter Sauce
  (see page 164), warmed
1 Roasted Red Pepper, finely diced
  (see page 174)
1 tablespoon coriander leaves,
  freshly chopped

about 100 g (4 oz) each. Cover with another sheet of greaseproof paper, then wrap clingfilm over them. Place the cakes in the freezer and allow them to freeze hard, preferably overnight.

Once frozen, prepare three shallow trays thus: Sift the flour into the first tray. Break the eggs and whisk them in the second tray. Half fill the third tray with breadcrumbs.

Remove the Fishcakes from the freezer, knocking any frost from them. Add two or three fishcakes to the first tray and coat them with flour, shaking off any excess. Then transfer the fishcakes to the second tray and coat well in the egg.

Finally, plonk them into the breadcrumbs, covering them thoroughly. Repeat this process with the rest of the cakes and refreeze them if not serving immediately.

Pre-heat the oven to 120°C/250°F/Gas Mark ½.

Heat a small frying pan until hot, then fill it one third full with oil and allow it to heat up for one or two minutes. Place the Fishcakes in the pan and shallow fry them for three or four minutes or until nicely golden in colour. Turn over and repeat on the other side, then, using tongs or a spatula, place the fishcakes onto a baking sheet covered with a double thickness kitchen roll.

Place the tray into a low oven for 45 minutes. This will complete the defrosting process. They will keep at this temperature for three or four hours without spoiling.

When you are ready, place the salad leaves in a bowl and add the seasoning, olive oil and lemon juice. Toss and coat all the leaves. Have four warmed plates ready and pile the leaves into the centre of each.

Add the diced pepper and coriander to the warmed Nage Butter Sauce. Give it a good whizz with a hand blender, check the seasoning for taste, then spoon it around each plate. Lay a fishcake on top of each salad pile and serve.

MARINATED ROAST LANGOUSTINES WITH CRISPY VEGETABLES AND SOY AND LIME SAUCE

I got the idea for this dish after eating it in a Chinese restaurant, where I was surprised at how much extra flavour langoustines have when you cook them with their shells on. So much so, that you need only use extra marinade for this dish instead of a sauce.

Langoustines are not at their best in summer. It is important to buy them alive, because dead langoustine taste like cotton wool and spoil very quickly. You should be able to buy them from a good fish-monger or you can obtain them by mail order from Loch Fyne Oysters (Tel: 01499 600264).

Pre-heat the oven to 150°C/300°F/Gas Mark 2.

For the Marinade, mix all the ingredients to-gether in a small mixing bowl. Set it aside until required.

For the Langoustines, pull the heads from them whilst still alive, then remove the centre vein. Do this by clasping the centre fin of the tail between your thumb and forefinger, twist and then pull, bringing the whole intestinal tract with it. This only works if the langoustines are alive and very fresh. Alternatively, get your fishmonger to do it.

Lay the tails belly down on a chopping board and, using a large, sharp knife, cut them in half along their length taking out any veins that are left behind. Place the halves shell-side down on a tray and sprinkle over half of the marinade. Leave for a minimum of 30 minutes and a maximum of three hours.

For the Crispy Vegetables, peel, top and tail the carrot. Wipe, top and tail the courgette. Then, using your potato peeler, cut as many long, thin slices as you can from both of them. They should be like ribbons. Leave them on kitchen paper.

In a deep pan, heat the sunflower oil until it is

FOR THE MARINADE:

1 tablespoon light Soy Sauce
1 tablespoon Nam Plas (Thai fish sauce)
1 red chilli, de-seeded and very finely chopped
Juice and zest from 1 lime
120 ml (4 fl oz) olive oil
½ teaspoon Chilli Oil (see page 169)
Maldon salt
2 teaspoons chopped fresh coriander

FOR THE LANGOUSTINES AND VEGETABLES:

20 large langoustines
1 medium carrot
1 medium courgette
Sunflower oil for frying

SERVES FOUR

LEFT: Marinated Roast
Langoustines with Crispy
Vegetables and Soy and Lime
Sauce (page 25). RIGHT: Filo
Basket of Mussels with Bacon
and Brie (page 39).

a medium temperature (150°C, 300°F) and deep fry the carrot until crisp (*i.e.* when the oil stops bubbling, but the carrot still has its colour). Remove it with a slotted spoon and drain on a tray lined with kitchen roll. Now do the same with the courgette, allowing them to brown slightly around the edges. (This can be done up to three hours in advance).

To serve, place the carrot and courgette ribbons into the oven, still on the tray but with the kitchen roll removed. Heat a large frying pan until it is very hot. Add a little sunflower oil and then quickly add half the langoustines. Stir fry them for two to three minutes until nicely browned, season with a little salt, white pepper and a squeeze of lime juice.

Remove the langoustine from the pan onto a tray before repeating with the remaining langoustines. Pour any pan juices into the remaining marinade. Keep everything warm.

Arrange ten of the langoustine halves on each warm plate, flesh side up and tails pointing to the centre of the plate. Pile a quarter of the Crispy Vegetables in the centre of the langoustines and drizzle the remaining marinade around the tails.

Repeat with the other three plates and serve.

LINGUINE WITH LANGOUSTINES, PARMESAN, BASIL, TOASTED PINE KERNELS AND EXTRA VIRGIN OLIVE OIL

All the preparation for this can be done well in advance and it's dead easy to serve. It is delicious cold, and also works well without the langoustines, making a very tasty vegetarian starter. If you can't get langoustine, defrosted frozen prawns will do.

Prepare the langoustine as described on page 25. Bring a large pot, half-filled with 1.75 litres (3 pints) of water to the boil. Add all the langoustine tails to the pan, bring back to the boil and cook for three minutes. Remove them with a slotted spoon, refresh in cold water and allow them to cool. Shell the langoustines by squeezing the edges of the shell together until you hear a crack then pull the edges apart, releasing the meat.

Place the cooked linguine into a large pan. Add the toasted pine nut kernels and langoustines. Season with the salt and pepper.

Pour the olive oil into a small pan and warm through. Crush the garlic with the flat blade of a heavy knife, sprinkle some salt over it and mash it together with the flat blade of the knife until it's like a paste. Add it to the olive oil, along with the basil and a good squeeze of lemon juice. Mix thoroughly and pour it into the pasta.

If you're preparing well in advance, this is the point at which the pasta may be set aside and kept for up to 12 hours.

To serve, heat the pasta on a medium heat for four to five minutes, stirring so that it doesn't stick to the bottom. Once it's hot, check the seasoning.

Tip everything into a big, warmed serving bowl and scatter over some Parmesan shavings and the basil and help yourselves!

900 g (2 lb) langoustine (or 100 g/4 oz prawns, cooked and peeled)
175 g (6 oz) linguine, cooked as per the instructions on packet, then cooled in cold water and drained
25 g (1 oz) pine nut kernels, toasted in moderate oven until lightly browned (160°C/325°F/Gas Mark 3 for five to six minutes)
25 g (1 oz) fresh Parmesan, grated
1 clove garlic
Lemon juice
15 g (½ oz) fresh basil, roughly chopped
Fresh ground white pepper
Maldon salt
2 tablespoons extra virgin olive oil

Parmesan shavings
Chopped basil

SERVES FOUR

LEFT: Fettucine of Monkfish and Mussels with a Curry and Coriander Velouté (page 40).
RIGHT: Warm Salad of Scallops and Carrot with a Sauternes Sauce (page 32).

WARM SALAD OF SCALLOPS AND CARROT WITH A SAUTERNES SAUCE

The common thread to the main ingredients in this dish is sweetness, and this needs to be balanced by the Vinaigrette dressing on the salad leaves. The colours are pretty and it's relatively easy to make, provided you get good quality scallops.

Sauterne is a sweet wine, but you could substitute almost any other high quality dessert wine.

175 g (6 oz) mixed salad leaves
250 ml (8 fl oz) sauternes (or other dessert wine)
75 g (3 oz) unsalted butter, cold and diced
Lemon juice
1 large carrot, peeled and grated
2 tablespoons sunflower oil
12 plump scallops, shelled and cleaned
1 tablespoon Vinaigrette (see page 170)
Maldon salt
Fresh ground white pepper

SERVES FOUR

Tear and pick over the washed and dried salad leaves into 2.5 cm (1 in) pieces, then place them in a mixing bowl until ready to use.

Put the sauternes into a small saucepan and bring it to the boil. On a high heat, reduce it by 80% to 50 ml (2 fl oz), then whisk in 50 g (2 oz) of the butter. Season and add half a teaspoon of lemon juice. Keep it warm.

In another small saucepan, heat the remaining butter with the grated carrot, one teaspoon of lemon juice and some seasoning. Stir from time to time with a fork and cook for five minutes. Keep it warm.

Heat a frying pan until it is hot. Add the sunflower oil and then the scallops. Gently fry them for one minute on each side, then remove them to a tray. Season with a little salt, pepper and lemon juice. Keep them warm.

To serve, add the Vinaigrette to the salad leaves with a little seasoning and toss lightly to coat the leaves. Divide them into equal piles on four plates, placing a bed of the hot, grated carrot alongside. Place three scallops on each carrot bed.

Add any juices left on the tray from the scallops to the still warm Sauternes Sauce. Taste to check seasoning and then spoon the sauce over the scallops.

They're ready to go.

FETTUCINE OF SCALLOPS WITH MINT, CHILLI AND CORIANDER

Two of my favourite ingredients — scallops and fresh pasta. The zing of the chilli, mint and coriander combine together to give this dish a wonderful oriental feel.

If using bought pasta, prepare to package instructions, cool in cold water, drain and then set aside.

Slice the scallops in half horizontally. Place them on a tray, cover in clingfilm and leave them in your fridge until they're needed.

Place the prepared pasta into a large pan. Add the mint, coriander, chilli and zest of lime and season lightly. At this point the pasta may be set aside and kept for up to 12 hours.

Warm the Nage Butter Sauce through.

Heat a frying pan through until hot. Add a tablespoon of sunflower oil and half the scallops. Cook them until a brown edge appears round the scallops. Now remove them and place them seared side up on a metal tray. Repeat with the rest of the scallops before seasoning them with salt, pepper and lime juice. Keep them warm.

Place the pasta pan on a hot stove and add the Nage Butter Sauce, carefully stirring until heated through. Taste and adjust the seasoning.

Lay out four serving plates. Divide equal portions of pasta between them and place the scallops around the edges. Dust over with the chives.

Serve.

100 g (4 oz) fresh fettucine (see page 172), cooked (or use bought fettucine, same amount)

12 plump scallops, shelled, cleaned and with roe removed

1 tablespoon mint leaves, shredded

1 heaped tablespoon coriander leaves

¼ red chilli, de-seeded and finely diced

Zest of ½ lime

150 ml (5 fl oz) Nage Butter Sauce (see page 164)

Sunflower oil to fry

1 tablespoon chives, chopped or snipped

Maldon salt

Fresh ground white pepper

Juice of 1 lime

SERVES FOUR

Mousseline of pike with a tomato and chervil butter sauce

Pike is a wonderful, delicately-flavoured freshwater fish, abundant in many Scottish lochs. It isn't used very much, possibly because of its rather complicated bone structure, which often means that the fillets become broken up during removal. So it's lucky, then, that pike makes great mousseline.

450 g (1 lb) pike fillets, boned and skinned
1 whole egg, size 3
450 ml (15 fl oz) double cream
1 tablespoon lemon juice
Cayenne pepper
150 ml (5 fl oz) Nage Butter Sauce (see page 164)
2 ripe plum Tomatoes Concasse (see page 171)
1 tablespoon chervil, chopped
Maldon salt
6 butter lined cooking moulds (dariole or 100 ml/3½ fl oz/No. 2 ramekins)

SERVES SIX

If serving immediately, pre-heat the oven to 190°C/375°F/Gas Mark 5

Break down the pike fillets in a food processor for one to two minutes. When it is smooth and thick (you may need to scape down the sides from time to time), add the egg and whizz the mixture for a further one to two minutes.

Scrape the fish out into a stainless steel sieve and force it through. (This prevents any sinew getting into the mix.) Transfer the pike to a shallow metal bowl and refrigerate for two hours.

Remove it from the fridge and place the metal bowl into another bowl (of similar size or slightly wider) half-filled with ice (this keeps the temperature of the fish low and helps prevent the mousseline from splitting).

Gradually start working in the cream a little at a time with a wooden spoon. The consistency you're aiming for is to be as soft as possible, but still keeping its shape in the bowl. At this point, add a little more cream and season the salt directly onto it. This prevents the salt making direct contact with the fish, which would lead to graininess in the mousse. Quickly fold the salted cream in, add the cayenne pepper and lemon juice to season.

Check the seasoning and consistency. (It should be smooth, but still holding its shape.) Divide the mousseline between the buttered moulds, tapping out any air.

If not cooking immediately, cover each filled mould with clingfilm and refrigerate the mousseline until you are ready to cook them. They will keep for a maximum of eight hours.

To serve, place the Nage Butter Sauce into a small pan and warm it through. Now place the moulds into a roasting tin and pour in enough hot water to come halfway up the outsides of the moulds. Place the tray into the pre-heated oven until very slightly risen on top. This should take about 12 minutes.

Check the mousselines are cooked by placing a sharp, slim knife into the centre of the mousse and then hold the tip of the blade against your lower lip. It should feel warm. It pays to check that all the mousselines will part company with the moulds prior to starting to serve. Any sticky ones will need help with a sharp knife slipped between mould and mousse. However, if the moulds are properly buttered this shouldn't happen.

Now prepare to serve the mousseline by laying out six warmed plates. To release the mousse, give the mould a quick shake, then, holding it with a clean tea towel to prevent burnt fingers, turn the mould upside down onto the plate. Do the same with the others.

Add the Tomatoes Concasse and chervil to the hot Nage Butter Sauce and then spoon the mixture over the mousselines.

Serve.

LIME, HONEY AND MINT MARINATED SCALLOPS WITH A SALAD OF HERBS

In this dish, the scallops are served nearly 'raw'. I say 'nearly', because the acidity of the lime partly 'cooks' the scallops. However, in order for this to happen the scallops have to be very fresh and thinly sliced. You could also use another firm fleshed fish for this, such as turbot, salmon or halibut.

12 plump scallops, thinly sliced

FOR THE MARINADE:
Zest and juice of 1 lime
1 teaspoon clear honey
A few drops of Chilli Oil (see page 169)
½ teaspoon Maldon salt, crushed
2 turns fresh ground white pepper
6 mint leaves, shredded
1 teaspoon Nam Plas (Thai fish sauce)
10 g (¼ oz) shredded Japanese picked ginger (optional)
1 tablespoon olive oil

FOR THE SALAD:
80 g (3 oz) sprigs of chervil, coriander, dill, chives, tarragon, sorrel, baby spinach, mâche, mixed (or whatever is available)

Mix all the marinade ingredients (keeping back a little lime juice) in one bowl and place the mixed herb salad in another bowl. Refrigerate them both until needed.

Thirty minutes prior to serving, add the sliced scallops to the marinade and mix well.

When you are ready to serve, season the herbs and dress them with a little olive oil and some more lime juice.

Arrange the scallops on cold serving plates. Divide the salad of herbs between them and spoon on a little of the remaining marinade.

CRAB AND PARMESAN SOUFFLÉ WITH MINT HOLLANDAISE

This is a savoury soufflé. Straightforward to make and, as always, the secret of success lies in the preparation. I must confess to using frozen crab meat. It's nearly as good as fresh and a lot easier than cracking crustaceans open with your bare hands. Use Scottish crabmeat if you can get it.

The Mint Hollandaise has to be made no more than one hour before it's needed.

Take six 150-ml (¼-pint) ramekins (size 1) and put them in your fridge before starting. This makes it easier to line them with butter.

Pre-heat the oven to 200°C/400°F/Gas Mark 6.

To make the soufflé base, melt the butter in a small pan but don't let it brown. Add the flour and mix well with a wooden spoon for two minutes. Grab a whisk, add the milk and bring it to a simmer, whisking all the time. Cook for a further ten minutes, then remove from the heat. Allow it to cool slightly before beating in the egg yolks, the Parmesan and the seasoning. Leave it to one side. (If you have any problems with lumps, force the mixture through a sieve and hey presto – no more lumps.)

The Hollandaise ingredients make eight portions, but that's because it isn't easy to make a smaller quantity when hand whisking – which is compulsory for good Hollandaise.

So, place the egg yolks in a metal bowl small enough to fit over a pan of simmering water. Melt the butter in another pan and then pour it into a jug. Put the egg bowl over the simmering water and add one tablespoon of hot water to the yolks. Start whisking until the yolks thicken enough to leave a visible trace on the surface of the mix (i.e. you should see a trail of egg yolk if you lift the whisk out of the bowl. This will take about five to seven minutes.

FOR THE SOUFFLÉ:

25 g (1 oz) unsalted butter (plus a little to line ramekins)
25 g (1 oz) plain flour
300 ml (10 fl oz) full cream milk
3 egg yolks, size 3
50 g (2 oz) fresh Parmesan, grated
5 egg whites, size 3
175 g (6 oz) defrosted or fresh crabmeat
25 g (1 oz) Breadcrumbs (see page 173)
Maldon salt
White pepper
Lemon juice

FOR THE HOLLANDAISE:

3 egg yolks, size 3
1 tablespoon hot water
175 g (6 oz) butter, melted
Juice of ¼ lemon
Seasoning
1 tablespoon mint, chopped

SERVES SIX

Continue to whisk as you pour in the melted butter in a slow, steady stream. The yolks should absorb all of the butter and have a beautiful, velvety texture. Now add the lemon juice and some salt and a little pepper, tasting and adjusting if necessary. Keep the Hollandaise warm for up to one hour until you are ready to serve. Remove the ramekins from your fridge and grease the insides with butter before coating them with the breadcrumbs. (It helps if the butter is at room temperature). Place the ramekins on a baking sheet and put them back into the fridge until you need them.

To serve, place the egg whites into the mixing bowl of an electric food mixer and whisk at full speed, adding a pinch of salt and a squeeze of lemon juice. Continue whisking until the whites are nice and light, *i.e.* when you can shape them into a soft peak. (A soft peak bends gently. If it stands straight and stiff, it's a 'stiff' peak.) Do not overwhisk here, if in doubt stop.

Place the soufflé base mix into another mixing bowl and mix in the crab meat with a wooden spoon.

Now mix one quarter of the whites into the soufflé base and work well with your spoon to loosen up the mix. Fold the remaining whites in gently, so as not to knock too much air out of it. It's the trapped air which makes the soufflé rise. A plastic spatula is best for this part.

Spoon the mix into the ramekins, bringing it level with the top but taking care not to get any on the rims. Give each ramekin a tap on the bottom – there's no need to smooth the tops. Place in the oven and set a timer for 15–20 minutes. The soufflés should be well risen and golden on top. They'll be a bit cracked, but this is okay.

Place each ramekin in the centre of a serving plate and serve the Hollandaise in a separate jug, allowing your guests to pour on as much as they like. If all's well, you'll get a wee round of applause from them. (The guests that is, not the soufflés!)

FILO BASKET OF MUSSELS WITH BACON AND BRIE

This dish was once by far the most popular starter at Braeval. So much so, I got fed up cooking it and stopped making it about three years ago, but customers still ask me for the recipe. So here it is.

If you are using cultivated mussels, soak them in cold water for 30 minutes, drain and pull off the beards. If using estuary mussels, you may need to scrub them to remove the sand from the shells, as well as soaking them.

For the Filo Baskets, pre-heat the oven to 190°C/ 375°F/Gas Mark 5.

Take three squares of the filo pastry and place the first one down on a surface (a chopping board will do) and brush with clarified butter. Turn the next square through 30 degrees, and place on top of the first before brushing with the butter. Turn the remaining one a further 30 degrees (thus creating a 'star' shape) and brush again with the butter.

Ease the star, butter-side down, into a buttered No. 1 size ramekin, the star points facing up. Push down well and prick the bottom with a fork. Repeat for the five other baskets. You should now have six filo-lined ramekins. Bake them in the pre-heated oven for five to six minutes until shaped and slightly golden. Remove them from oven and lift the baskets out of ramekins. Turn the baskets upside down and replace them on a baking sheet and return to oven to cook for a further four to five minutes until evenly brown. Leave to cool on a wire rack. These will keep for up to 12 hours.

For the Mussel Filling, choose a pan with a tight fitting lid. Heat it dry and then pour the mussels in. Add 85 ml (3 fl oz) of wine, place the lid on and cook until the mussels open (this takes about five minutes). Do not overcook and discard any that don't open in this time.

FOR THE FILO BASKETS:

18 × 15 cm (6 in) square sheets of filo pastry (cut from 3 leaves)

75 ml (3 fl oz) Clarified Butter (see page 175)

FOR THE MUSSEL FILLING:

2.25 kg (5 lb) mussels, rinsed, scrubbed and de-bearded

300 ml (10 fl oz) dry white wine

50 g (2 oz) unsalted butter

1 onion, finely chopped

2 cloves garlic, crushed and finely chopped

150 ml (¼ pint) reserved mussel juice

300 ml (½ pint) Fish Stock (see page 161)

Juice of ½ a lemon

150 ml (5 fl oz) double cream

3 rashers smoked back bacon, grilled and drained of the fat

Maldon salt

Fresh ground white pepper

Pinch of sugar

150 g (5 oz) ripe Brie, rind
removed

TO GARNISH:
225 g (8 oz) salad leaves
4 tablespoons Vinaigrette (see page
170)

SERVES SIX

Drain in a collander set over a bowl, then shell the mussels before straining the juice carefully through a double muslin or chinois.

Melt the butter in a saucepan and sweat the chopped onion and garlic until soft. Add the mussel juice, fish stock and the rest of the white wine. Reduce it to a fifth of the volume.

Now add the lemon juice, cream and seasoning and reduce again until it is very thick and sticky. Add the bacon and mussels and heat through, checking your seasoning as you go.

Place the mixture into the filo baskets. Top each one with a square of Brie and pop them into a hot oven for three minutes.

Serve the baskets on individual plates surrounded by dressed salad leaves.

FETTUCINE OF MONKFISH AND MUSSELS WITH A CURRY AND CORIANDER VELOUTÉ

This dish is seriously tasty. The meaty texture of the monkfish is a perfect foil for the squidgy mussels. The coriander has a natural affinity for both the pasta *and* the fish. Add the curry paste cautiously, however, since it should be very much a background flavour.

750 g (1½ lb) mussels, cleaned and
de-bearded
120 ml (4 fl oz) white wine
25 g (1 oz) unsalted butter
2 shallots, finely diced
½ teaspoon medium curry paste
4 button mushrooms, finely sliced

Firstly, cook the mussels in a pan with a tight fitting lid and large enough for them to only half fill it. Heat the pan until hot, rattle in the mussels and then the wine. With the lid on, shake the pan. Cook until all the mussels have opened. (This should take about three minutes).

As soon as they're ready, set a sieve or collander over a bowl and pour in the mussels. Strain the juice caught in the bowl and reserve 175 ml (6 fl oz) of it. Shell the mussels and put them to one side.

For the Sauce, melt the butter in a small saucepan. Add the shallots and the curry paste and cook for two minutes over a medium heat. Add the mushrooms and cook for a further two minutes. Now add the mussel juice and reduce over a high heat until the liquid becomes thick and foamy (this takes about 10–15 minutes).

Add the cream and bring back to the boil. Season with a touch of lemon juice. You shouldn't need any salt, since the mussel juices are quite salty. Keep it warm.

To cook the monkfish, heat a frying pan until it is very hot. Add the sunflower oil and fry the monk fillet until it is nicely browned (this will take about four minutes). Season with salt, pepper and lemon juice. Remove the pan from the heat and leave to rest in a warm place whist you prepare the next bit . . .

. . . which is the pasta. Put your pre-cooked fettucine in a saucepan, add the mussels and coriander, then pour on the sauce. Heat it through gently and check your seasoning.

To serve, divide the pasta and mussel mixture between four warm serving plates. Carve the monkfish into 12 slices, laying three slices of monkfish on each plate. Now eat it!

175 ml (6 fl oz) reserved mussel
  juice
175 ml (6 fl oz) double cream
Lemon juice
2 tablepoons sunflower oil
225 g (8 oz) piece of monkfish fillet
  trimmed of all skin
225 g (8 oz) fettucine, cooked
12 tablespoons coriander, chopped
Maldon salt
Fresh ground white pepper

_____

SERVES FOUR

Baked Fillet of Sole with
Vegetables (page 44).

BAKED FILLET OF SOLE WITH VEGETABLES

This is a nice, simple starter which, with the addition of a few boiled new potatoes, also makes a great lunch on its own. You can use a variety of different vegetables, as long as they're all cut small, to facilitate faster cooking. Really fresh sole is not snow white – it should have a greyish tinge. If it *is* snow white, it's been bleached, usually by the fish processors. So ask your fishmonger to cut your fillets from a whole sole.

4 × 100 g (4 oz) lemon or grey sole
   fillets, skinned and boned
40 g (1½ oz) unsalted butter
Lemon juice
1 tablespoon white wine (or water)
150 ml (5 fl oz) Nage Butter Sauce
   (see page 164)
4 asparagus stalks, peeled and each cut
   into 8 pieces
1 small courgette, finely sliced
1 small carrot, peeled and very finely
   sliced
12 snap peas, each cut into 4
24 broad beans, shelled and blanched
   for two minutes in salted boiling
   water
1 plum Tomatoes Concasse (see page
   171)
Maldon salt
Fresh ground white pepper
1 tablespoon chervil, roughly chopped

Pre-heat the oven to 230°C/450°F/Gas Mark 8.

Season the sole fillets, fold them in half and place them on a buttered baking sheet. Put a teaspoon of butter and a squeeze of lemon juice on top of each sole. Pour the wine (or water) onto the baking sheet and then place it in the oven for four minutes.

While the sole is cooking, heat through the Nage Butter Sauce in a pan and add all the vegetables except for the tomatoes. Cook them gently for two to three minutes.

Warm four shallow bowls and remove the sole from the oven. It should be just cooked and no more.

Divide the vegetable sauce between the serving bowls and place a sole fillet on top of each. Scatter the Tomatoes Concasse and chervil over the top.

Eat at once.

SERVES FOUR

BAKED FILLET OF HALIBUT, SPAGHETTI OF CARROT AND A DILL BUTTER SAUCE

This is a relatively easy and colourful starter which, if the quantities were increased by about one quarter, would also make a good main dish. Get your fishmonger to fillet the halibut for you and if you can't get fillets, halibut steaks would do although you'd have to increase the cooking time very slightly depending on their thickness (probably about one minute). For more words of wisdom on halibut, see page 74.

Pre-heat the oven to 230°C/450°F/Gas Mark 8.

Take 20 g (¾ oz) of the butter and smear it over the base of a roasting tin large enough to hold the four fish fillets. Place the fillets into the tin and dot them with pinch sized bits of the remaining butter.

Add one tablespoon of water to the tin, cover with clingfilm and refrigerate the fillets until you are ready to cook.

Place the grated carrot in a small pan. Add the remaining butter, a squeeze of lemon juice, a pinch of salt and three turns of the white pepper. Keep to one side until ready to serve.

To serve, place the pan with the carrot on a low to medium heat and cook for five to six minutes, stirring occasionally. Keep it warm.

Take the halibut from the fridge, remove the clingfilm and season each fillet. Squeeze over two teaspoons of lemon juice and place the roasting tin into the oven, setting your timer for six minutes.

Pour the Nage Butter Sauce into a pan and heat it through.

Heat a large, dry saucepan until hot. Add the olive oil and quickly sautée the spinach leaves until just limp. Season them and add one teaspoon of lemon juice.

Divide the spinach over four warm plates. Take

4 × 100 g (4 oz) halibut fillets
50 g (2 oz) unsalted butter
1 medium carrot, peeled and grated
Juice of ½ a lemon
150 ml (5 fl oz) Nage Butter Sauce
  (see page 164)
1 tablespoon olive oil
75 g (3 oz) spinach leaves, picked
  and washed
1 heaped tablespoon dill, chopped
Maldon salt
Fresh ground white pepper

SERVES FOUR

the roasting tin from the oven and place a halibut fillet on each pile of spinach. Give the Nage Butter Sauce a last whisk, add the dill, check your seasoning and pour equally over each serving. Top each fish with equal quantities of the grated carrot, sprinkle on a little more dill and serve.

BRANDADE OF SALT COD WITH OLIVES AND CROÛTONS

This is a recent addition to my hoard of recipes, made at the request of a dinner guest who was the UK's largest producer of salt cod. He told me that 99% of the cod was exported, mainly to Portugal, and after tasting the Brandade, all I could think was — lucky Portuguese!

450 g (1 lb) salt cod fillet
175 ml (6 fl oz) full cream milk
3 cloves garlic, crushed
250 ml (8 fl oz) olive oil
175 g (6 oz) Mashed Potatoes (see page 127)
Juice of 1 lemon
Fresh ground black pepper
Olive Oil Croûtons (see page 175), around 4 slices
32 black olives, stoned and quartered
1 tablespoons chives, chopped
25 g (1 oz) fresh Parmesan, grated
Olive oil to serve

SERVES EIGHT

Soak the cod for 24 hours in several changes of cold water. Poach it in simmering water for six minutes, remove and allow to cool slightly. This makes it easier to pull the bones out using a pair of stout tweezers.

Place the milk, oil and crushed garlic into a small pan and warm it through. Pour into a jug and put to one side.

Put the de-boned cod and Mashed Potatoes into a food processor and whizz it until just smooth.

Take the milk and oil mix in the jug (yes, I know, it looks pretty disgusting) and pour it onto the cod and potato mix in a steady stream, whizzing all the while. Stop processing as soon as all the liquid is absorbed. Add the lemon juice and plenty of fresh ground black pepper before processing again for further 30 seconds.

Divide the Brandade amongst individual warmed serving dishes and scatter the croûtons, olives and Parmesan over the top. Sprinkle with chives and drizzle on a little more olive oil to serve.

The Brandade can be cooled and reheated — it keeps for about three days in the fridge.

SEARED FILLET OF JOHN DORY WITH CRUSHED POTATO AND CHIVE BUTTER SAUCE

A sadly underused fish, John Dory has lovely white flesh with nice big flakes and a fine sweet flavour. The crushed potato is *not* mash, as you will discover . . .

Pre-heat the oven to 220°C/425°F/Gas Mark 7.

Place the potatoes on a bed of sea salt in a roasting tray and bake in the oven for one and a half hours. Remove and then cut the baked potatoes in half. Using a teaspoon, dig out the cooked potato and put it into a mixing bowl. (You can keep the skins for making . . . erm . . . potato skins). Add the butter, shallots, spring onion and a little seasoning. Gently mix it together with a fork until all the melted butter has been absorbed and the potato is nice and lumpy. Keep it warm.

Heat a dry frying pan until it is hot. Add two tablespoons of sunflower oil and fry the John Dory until golden. The fillets need only be seared on one side and it's better to cook them two at a time rather than crowd the pan.

Remove the fillets from the pan and place them on a warmed metal tray, seared side up. Season with crushed salt, fresh ground white pepper and a good squeeze of lemon juice. Leave to rest in a warm place.

Have four warmed plates ready and heat the Nage Butter Sauce.

Spoon the potato mix onto the centre of each plate. Place a fish fillet on top of each little pile. Pour any lemony fish juices from the tray into the Nage Butter Sauce, add the chives, taste and check the seasoning.

Before pouring, you could give the sauce a quick blast with a hand blender to get it nice and frothy. When you are happy with it spoon it over the fish and serve with haste.

2 large baking potatoes
Sunflower oil (for frying)
4 × 100 g (4 oz) John Dory fillets
75 g (3 oz) unsalted butter, diced
2 shallots, very finely chopped
1 spring onion, finely chopped
Sea salt
Fresh ground white pepper
Lemon juice
150 g (5 oz) Nage Butter Sauce
1 tablespoon freshly chopped chives

SERVES FOUR

ROAST FILLET OF TROUT WITH A COMPOTE OF AVOCADO AND TOMATO IN A BASIL BUTTER SAUCE

Trout is a sadly underused fish which has a great combination of good flavour and fine texture. I use the fillets from large, farmed Scottish trout which I buy ready-skinned and boned. They represent great value for money. This was once a salmon dish and, if you want to ensure that trout remains underused, you could substitute with salmon.

FOR THE AVOCADO COMPOTE:

1 large, ripe avocado
2 ripe, plum Tomatoes Concasse
  (see page 171)
1 tablespoon extra virgin olive oil
Juice of half a lemon
Dash of Worcester Sauce
Dash of Tabasco
4 leaves of basil, finely chopped
Maldon salt
Fresh ground white pepper

FOR THE ROAST TROUT FILLET:

4 x 75 g (3 oz) thin (4 mm)
  escalopes of trout
Peanut or sunflower oil for frying
Lemon juice
150 g (5 oz) unsalted butter
150 ml (5 fl oz) Nage Butter Sauce
18 leaves basil, chopped
Maldon salt
Fresh ground white pepper

To make the Avocado Compote skin the avocado and chop into 1 cm (½ in) chunks. Mix the avocado with the Tomatoes Concasse. Add the remaining ingredients and mix well. This can now wait somewhere while you get on with the fishy bit . . .

Cut your fish escalopes diagonally with a good sharp knife. (Alternatively, get your fishmonger to do this before you leave the shop.)

Heat your frying pan until hot, pour on your oil and quickly fry the fish escalopes for approximately two minutes on one side only. Don't try to move the fish until you see a brown edge appear — a seared, dark appearance at the edges is perfect.

Remove the escalopes from the pan and place them on a warm metal tray, seared side up.

Squeeze the lemon juice over them and season with Maldon salt and fresh ground white pepper.

Lay out four warmed serving plates and divide the compote between the centre of the plates.

Add the basil to the Nage Butter Sauce. Check the seasoning and pour it around the compote.

Finally, place an escalope on top of each pile of compote and serve.

SERVES FOUR

PART THREE

OTHER STARTERS

PARFAIT OF CHICKEN LIVERS WITH CUMBERLAND SAUCE

This is a very rich and smooth chicken liver pâté (in effect a custard) and so needs a little care not to overcook it. Fresh chicken livers are fabulously tasty and cheap and the fruity Cumberland sauce perfectly complements the rich flavour of the parfait.

FOR THE PARFAIT:

450 g (1 lb) fresh chicken livers
8 egg yolks, size 3
425 g (15 oz) unsalted butter, melted
250 ml (8 fl oz) double cream
1 tablespoon port
1 tablespoon cognac
½ clove of garlic, crushed
1 teaspoon Maldon salt
12 turns white pepper

Dressed green salad to serve

FOR THE CUMBERLAND SAUCE:

500 g (18 oz) redcurrant jelly
250 ml (8 fl oz) ruby port
Juice and grated rind of 2 lemons
Juice and grated rind of 2 oranges
1 teaspoon ground cinnamon
2 teaspoons English mustard

MAKES 12 PARFAITS

Pre-heat the oven to 180°C/350°F/Gas Mark 4. Line a 450 g (1 lb) loaf tin with clingfilm and put it to one side.

Trim the chicken livers to remove any fat, sinew or gunky bits in general. Place in a liquidiser and add everything else but the melted butter. Liquidise until very smooth (about three minutes), then pour in the melted butter. The mix in the liquidiser should turn a pale pink colour. Keep whizzing for a further minute. Pour the mixture through a sieve into the lined loaf tin, letting the mixture come to the brim.

To protect the surface of the mix from burning, cover it with clingfilm, then place a double thickness of tinfoil over the top.

Place the loaf tin into a roasting tray and pour enough water into the tray to come halfway up the tin. Place in the oven and cook for 40 minutes.

After 40 minutes, the top should be slightly risen. At this stage, you need to test the mixture to see if it will set. To do this, remove it from oven and take off the tinfoil but not the clingfilm. Give the tin a wee shake. The centre of the parfait should wobble, but not the edges. If it's *all* wobbling, stick it back (replacing the foil) in the roasting tray and cook for a further five minutes in the oven.

If all is perfect however, lift the loaf tin from the tray and allow to cool. Once cooled, refrigerate overnight.

Next day, have a piece of wood, polystyrene or stiff card which is the same width as the loaf tin, but two inches (5 cm) or so longer. Cover this with tinfoil and remove the top layer of clingfilm from the Parfait, cutting away any excess clingfilm sticking to the edges of the tin.

Dip the whole tin into a basin of hot water (the water *nearly* reaching the top). Count to 20, then remove it and place the foil-covered board on top of the tin. Turn it upside down and lift off the tin and clingfilm, leaving you with the Parfait sitting on a serving board.

To make the Cumberland sauce, place all the ingredients into a saucepan and bring to the boil. Skim away the froth and reduce over a medium heat for approximately 30 minutes. Strain the sauce through a fine sieve and cool. When cold, it should have the consistency of runny honey.

This zingy, fruity sauce keeps for up to eight weeks in the fridge. I store mine in an old tomato sauce dispenser (a squeezy bottle), so that I can easily drizzle it around the plate.

To serve, use a metal spatula dipped in hot water to cut slices of parfait. Place each slice on a cold plate and garnish with a little dressed salad and a tablespoon of Cumberland Sauce.

You can re-clingfilm any remaining parfait and store in the fridge for up to one week.

FETTUCINE OF LIME, CHILLI AND GARLIC MARINATED CHICKEN WITH WHITE WINE AND BASIL

When this starter is served, it *always* draws praise. The flash-fried marinated chicken is versatile enough to go with either rice or salad, if you don't fancy pasta. You can use bought fettucine instead of fresh, but do try to get maize-fed chicken breasts or free range ones.

FOR THE MARINATED CHICKEN:

175 g (6 oz) fettucine, cooked
2 chicken breasts (maize-fed if possible)
Zest of 1 lemon
2 teaspoons Chilli Oil (see page 169)
2 teaspoons olive oil
1 clove garlic
2 tablespoons sunflower oil (for frying)
Maldon salt
Fresh ground white pepper
Juice of ½ lemon
Fresh Parmesan shavings for garnish

FOR THE SAUCE:

25 g (1 oz) unsalted butter
4 shallots, peeled and finely sliced
6 button mushrooms, sliced
½ clove garlic, crushed
1 bay leaf
1 sprig thyme
4 white peppercorns, crushed
250 ml (8 fl oz) white wine
85 ml (3 fl oz) double cream
8 large basil leaves
475 ml (16 fl oz) Chicken Stock (see page 162)

SERVES FOUR

You can marinate the chicken between one to six hours prior to use.

Remove skin and sinew from each breast and pull off the long breast fillet. Using a sharp knife, cut thin – 3 mm (⅛ in) – slices of chicken across the grain. Cut each fillet into three pieces and you should have 25 to 30 pieces of chicken.

Place them in a small bowl and, using a zester, scrape off the lemon rind directly onto the chicken. Add the Chilli Oil, the olive oil and four turns of white pepper. Cover with clingfilm and refrigerate until you are ready to cook it.

You can make the sauce up to two days ahead.

Melt the butter in a saucepan and add the shallots, mushrooms, garlic, bay, thyme and pepper and lightly fry until golden. Add the wine and reduce over a high heat until the pan is nearly dry.

Add the Chicken Stock and reduce it by two thirds. Add the cream and bring it back to the boil. Pour the whole contents of the pan through a sieve into a jug, using a ladle to press and force out all of the sauce. Check the seasoning and reserve the sauce in the fridge until needed.

To serve, heat a large frying pan or wok until it is hot. While that's happening, warm the Sauce through in a medium-sized saucepan, then add the pasta. Check the seasoning and gently warm the pasta through in the Sauce.

Add the sunflower oil to the frying pan and dump the chicken pieces in it. Stir-fry until nicely browned and season it with crushed sea salt. At the last moment, squeeze over the juice of half a lemon and shake the pan to evenly coat the chicken pieces.

Tip the chicken out onto a double layer of kitchen roll to drain.

Now the pasta. Finely chop the basil and add to the pasta, stir well, then divide the pasta between four warmed serving bowls. Divide the chicken pieces over the pasta and scatter over a few shavings of Parmesan.

It's ready to serve.

POACHED LEEKS WITH ROAST CHICKEN LIVERS, ROCKET, PARMESAN, OLIVE OIL AND BALSAMIC VINEGAR

A variation on the classic leeks vinaigrette. Of course, you could just serve the leeks with some Parmesan and the dressing, but you'd be missing out on the fabby flavours, textures and temperature contrasts when served with the warm livers (and I surely do love my temperature contrasts).

Have handy a bowl of iced water.

Bring a large pan of salted water to the boil. Cut the leeks into 12 cm (2½ inch) lengths and chuck them into the boiling water. Poach them until tender (this will take about eight minutes). Lift them out with a slotted spoon and bung them straight into the iced water (this stops the cooking and at the same time retains the colour).

Once cooled (about five minutes later), remove and gently wring out the excess water. Place the leeks into a shallow serving dish, pour the Vinaigrette over them. Season with a touch of salt and 10 turns of the white pepper. Leave it for at least 30 minutes to marinate. (I've even, on occasion, left them overnight, and although they lose a bit of colour, they still taste bonzer!)

To serve, heat a frying pan until hot, splash in three tablespoons of olive oil and drop in the chicken livers. Fry until nicely browned, then turn and season with salt and pepper. Keep frying until the other sides have a nice bit of colour on them. (This should take about four minutes cooking time.)

Pull the pan off the heat, lift out the livers and place them on top of the leeks.

Fling the rocket leaves into the frying pan and

6 long, thin, straight leeks, trimmed and washed
3 tablespoons Vinaigrette (see page 170)
6 tablespoons olive oil
175 g (6 oz) chicken livers, trimmed
15g (½ oz) rocket leaves
25 g (1 oz) fresh Parmesan shavings
1 tablespoon balsamic vinegar
Maldon salt
Fresh ground white pepper

SERVES FOUR

LEFT: Poached Leeks with Roast Chicken Livers, Rocket, Parmesan, Olive Oil and Balsamic Vinegar (page 53).
RIGHT: Terrine of Chicken and Leeks Wrapped in Parma Ham (page 64).

coat them in the hot juices. Tip them out onto the livers and scatter the Parmesan over the top.

Finally, drizzle over the remaining oil and the balsamic vinegar. Serve in the dish and let the guests help themselves. Or, if you want to be posh, cut each leek into three bits, and place equally on four serving plates. Then divide up the rest of the ingredients and hand it round already plated.

It's a good idea to have plenty of fresh bread handy.

PAN FRIED LAMBS' KIDNEYS WITH GRAIN MUSTARD AND SAFFRON BASMATI RICE

You either like kidneys or you don't. Personally (and you know what's coming next) I *love* lambs kidneys. And I want them pink inside, not grey, with that squidgy texture and heavenly flavour. Mustard is a natural partner and the basmati rice has a lovely perfume which blends well with the saffron.

175 g (6 oz) basmati rice
6 lambs kidneys
1 teaspoon sunflower oil
25 g (1 oz) unsalted butter
2 tablespoons cognac
300 ml (10 fl oz) Beef or Chicken
  Stock (see page 162)
120 ml (4 fl oz) double cream
Pinch of saffron strands
1½ teaspoons grain mustard
  (Meaux is good)
1 teaspoon chives, chopped
Maldon salt
Fresh ground white pepper

SERVES FOUR

First, following the directions on the packet, cook the rice adding the saffron to the cooking water. Drain and keep it warm.

Have a large, warmed plate handy and heat a large frying pan until it is hot.

Halve the kidneys lengthwise and through the gristly bit. Remove the skin and gristle and season the kidney halves with salt and pepper. Drop the oil into the hot pan and add six kidney halves, cut side down, and half of the butter. Fry until brown. Turn over and repeat. (This should take about four minutes.)

Lift the kidneys out and onto the warmed plate. Add the remaining butter to the frying pan and cook the rest of the kidneys.

When all the kidneys have been fried and removed from the pan, slosh the cognac into it. It should boil off straight away. Add the stock and reduce quickly by about two thirds.

Add the cream and bring back to the boil. Pour the kidney juices from the warmed plate into the frying pan and check the sauce for seasoning.

You can hold off serving here for a bit of vino and a chat to your pals (I presume you're not eating them all yourself).

When you're ready to serve, put the kidneys back into the sauce and warm them through. Divide the rice between four plates, making a nice pile in the centre. Place three kidney halves on top of each pile, spoon over the sauce, dust with the chives.

Now serve.

GÂTEAU OF ROAST VEGETABLES WITH PARMA HAM, PARMESAN, ROCKET AND TOMATO VINAIGRETTE

This little blast of Provence can brighten up a gloomy winter's day. The vegetables and the rocket are available all year round. If you leave out the Parma ham you have a colourful vegetarian starter. This is ideal for a dinner party, since the gâteau can be made well in advance.

Wipe the aubergine, top and tail it, and cut into eight discs. Lightly salt the slices and leave them to drain for 10 minutes in a sieve. Wash and drain them again. Quarter the red pepper.

Wipe the courgette, top and tail it and, cutting across at an angle of 45 degrees, cut it into 8 slices.

Heat a frying pan large enough to hold the aubergine slices and add the sunflower oil. Pat the aubergine slices dry on a clean teatowel, then carefully add them to the frying pan, watching out for hot oil splashes.

Fry them until they are golden brown (about five

1 small aubergine
1 fat, ripe Roasted Red Pepper
  (see page 174)
1 medium courgette
150 ml (5 fl oz) sunflower oil
Juice of ½ lemon
50 ml (2 fl oz) olive oil
2 very ripe plum tomatoes,
  quartered
4 Home Dried Tomatoes (see
  page 166)

4 slices of Parma ham
25 g (1 oz) Parmesan shavings
15 g (½ oz) rocket leaves
½ teaspoon balsamic vinegar
Maldon salt
Fresh ground white pepper

SERVES FOUR

to seven minutes should do), then turn them and fry the other side. When they're done, the aubergines should feel light and firm (not heavy and soggy!)

The oil should still be clean, so carefully add the courgette slices and fry them until nicely browned (it will take about two to three minutes approximately). Cook them on one side only. Remove them from the pan and place them in a mixing bowl. Add the four red pepper quarters, then the lemon juice and one tablespoon of olive oil. Season with a little Maldon salt and four turns of pepper. Add the Home Dried Tomatoes and cover the bowl with clingfilm.

Allow it to cool, and the flavours to combine, for about an hour (although you could leave it overnight).

To make the tomato vinaigrette, place the tomatoes in a liquidiser with 25 ml (1 fl oz) of olive oil, a ½ teaspoon of salt and 3 turns of pepper. Give it a quick whizz to break down the tomatoes (it'll take about 45 seconds), then empty the liquid into a fine sieve. Force it through with a ladle, taste for seasoning and keep to one side until ready to serve.

When you're ready, make the gâteau by placing four of the aubergine slices on a tray. Get the courgette slices and dried tomatoes and place one of each, side by side, on each slice of aubergine. The red pepper goes on next, followed by the remaining aubergine slices and the last of the courgette.

To serve, remove the tray holding the gâteau from the fridge, take off the clingfilm and then lift each gâteau onto a serving plate. Spoon around 3 tablespoons of the tomato vinaigrette.

Dress the rocket leaves with the other 25 ml (1 fl oz) of olive oil. Lay out a strip of Parma ham and spread the rocket on it, followed by the Parmesan shavings and the vinegar, and roll up the ham.

Place the roll of Parma ham and rocket on top of the gâteau — and serve!

FETTUCINE OF ROASTED RED PEPPER, BLACK OLIVES AND CAPERS WITH PESTO

Easy to make and ideal for a dinner party (because all the hard work is done in advance), this Mediterranean dish is a fave — especially if you go for it and make your own pasta. If you don't have a pasta machine though, worry not — brought in, fresh stuff works nearly as well.

Cut the red pepper into 5 mm (¼ in) diced pieces. Mix them in a bowl with the olives, pasta, capers, lemon juice, the salt and pepper, rocket leaves, half of the fresh grated Parmesan, the Pesto and the Mediterranean Sauce Vierge. Check the seasoning. Divide the mixture carefully between four small pans, ensuring that all the ingredients are distributed evenly. This mixture can now be kept in the fridge for up to 12 hours prior to cooking.

To cook, heat the pans thoroughly over a medium heat. This takes about five minutes, during which you should stir each pan in turn to prevent sticking. If you don't have four small pans, then cook the pasta in one big pan and divide the portions out with a spoon.

When hot, tip the mixture into warmed serving bowls and top them with the remaining Parmesan.

Lastly, roughly shred the basil leaves and sprinkle them equally over the top.

1 × 150 g (5 oz) Roasted Red Pepper (see page 174)
12 best quality black olives, stoned and halved
240 g (8 oz) fettucine (or tagliatelle), cooked, cooled in cold water and drained
16 dry salted capers, rinsed
2 teaspoons lemon juice
2 teaspoons Maldon salt
¼ teaspoon fresh milled white pepper
20 g (¾ oz) small rocket leaves
1 heaped tablespoon Pesto (see page 000)
60 ml (2 fl oz) Mediterranean Sauce Vierge (see page 176)
15 g (½ oz) fresh Parmesan, grated
8 large basil leaves
1 tablespoon olive oil

SERVES FOUR

LASAGNE OF WILD MUSHROOMS AND BABY ASPARAGUS WITH CHERVIL BUTTER SAUCE

This vegetarian starter began life as a quickly knocked up dish for an unannounced vegetarian guest in the restaurant. I had pasta and asparagus from a starter and I added the mushrooms earmarked for the beef course. And you know what? She said it was the best dish she'd ever eaten! But I'll hang onto my ego – she might have meant the best she'd eaten all day. If you can't get baby asparagus, cut the regular stuff into 2.5 cm (1 in) slices.

100 g (4 oz) baby asparagus
25 g (1 oz) unsalted butter
175 g (6 oz) mixed wild mushrooms
   (e.g. chantarelle, trompette, cep,
   pied mouton, shitake, pleurotte,
   field – you could even use button),
   cleaned and sliced
175 ml (6 fl oz) Nage Butter Sauce
   (see page 164)
2 teaspoons light Soy Sauce
8 sheets lasagne (about 7 × 7 cm/3
   × 3 inches each), cooked (see
   page 172 about trimming)
2 tablespoons chervil, chopped (for
   garnish)
Lemon juice
Maldon salt
Fresh ground white pepper

SERVES FOUR

Bring a pan of salted water to the boil and throw in the baby asparagus. Cook it for one and a half minutes, then fish it out with a slotted spoon. Cool it in a bowl of cold water. Drain it and keep to one side.

Heat a frying pan until it's hot, then drop in the butter. As soon as the foaming butter browns, drop in the sliced mushrooms and stir them to coat. Cook for five to six minutes until lightly browned, then season with the salt, pepper and lemon juice. Tip everything into a bowl and keep to one side.

To serve, have a pan of simmering water ready. Heat the Nage Butter Sauce through and add the asparagus, the mushrooms and the Soy Sauce. Stir and warm it through.

Dump the pasta into the hot water for 90 seconds, then remove it with a slotted spoon and drain it on a clean teatowel.

Season the Nage and vegetable mix.

Into each of four pre-warmed serving bowls, place a sheet of pasta and, using a slotted spoon, divide half of the vegetable mix between the bowls. Cover each with the remaining four sheets of pasta, then spoon over the remaining vegetables.

Add the chervil to the remaining sauce, spoon it over and serve!

WARM SALAD OF DUCK BREAST WITH WILD RICE AND BLUEBERRIES

I am a particular fan of warm salads and I love the juiciness of the duck and blueberries here. The wild rice adds texture and contrast. Pick your salad leaves from a selection of oakleaf, lollo rosso, iceberg, little gem, curly endive, mâche and rocket. You'll need four handfuls of these leaves (175 g/6 oz).

Drain the wild rice and place in a saucepan. Add the bayleafs, garlic and thyme and just enough water to cover. Season to taste. Cook very slowly for 15 minutes on a medium heat until some of the rice has started to open. Drain it and put into a shallow dish. Cover with tin foil with a couple of holes pierced in it and keep warm.

Pick over and tear the salad leaves down to 2.5 cm (1 in) pieces. Place them in a mixing bowl and keep it in the fridge until ready to serve.

Heat a frying pan until it is hot. Now season the duck breasts on both sides with salt and pepper. Add the sunflower oil to the pan and then drop in the duck breasts, skin side up. Toss them in the butter and allow it to foam and swirl around the pan.

After two minutes, turn the duck breasts and cook for a further four minutes, this time skin side down. Now turn skin side up again and put the frying pan in a warm place to rest for up to one hour if preferred.

To serve, pop the frying pan back onto a low heat and gently warm it through (this will be about two to three minutes). In a bowl, season the salad leaves with salt and pepper.

Remove the duck breasts from the frying pan (they should be warm, not roasting hot). On a board, carve the duck as thinly as possible with a sharp carving knife. Add the thin slices of duck to the leaves along with any juices released during carving.

Now add the warm rice and gently mix every-

50 g (2 oz) wild rice, soaked overnight in 600 ml (1 pint) water
1 bay leaf
1 clove garlic
1 sprig thyme
2 × 175 g (6 oz) duck breasts
1 tablespoon sunflower oil
175 g (6 oz) mixed salad leaves (see the above introduction)
2 tablespoons Vinaigrette (see page 170)
50 g (2 oz) blueberries
25 g (1 oz) unsalted butter
25 g (1 oz) Olive Oil Croûtons (see page 175) (optional)
Maldon salt
Fresh ground pepper

SERVES FOUR

LEFT: Lasagne of Seared Salmon,
Samphire and Tomato with a
Frothy Herb Sauce (page 21).
RIGHT: Lasagne of Wild
Mushrooms and Baby
Asparagus with Chervil Butter
Sauce (page 60).

thing together. Combine the Vinaigrette and blue-berries with the oily pan juices and quickly warm it through for about 30 seconds. Pour this over the salad and toss well.

Divide the salad between four warmed serving plates. Scatter the Croûtons over and serve.

TERRINE OF CHICKEN AND LEEKS, WRAPPED IN PARMA HAM

This requires a fair degree of preparation and work, but it can all be done well in advance, leaving just the slicing of the terrine, come serving time. Leeks, chicken and Parma ham are an excellent combo of flavours and this is my favourite non-fishy terrine. Take a little care when layering the terrine, since you want to be able to see all the different layers in nice, straight lines.

This is good served with an olive oil and chervil sauce, which is incredibly simple to make.

FOR THE TERRINE:

7 thin slices Parma ham, large
  enough to wrap around the terrine
12 long straight leeks, whole
6 × 150–175 g (5–6 oz) chicken
  breasts, preferably maize-fed
2 egg yolks
440 ml (8 fl oz) double cream
1 teaspoon cooking salt
2 tablespoons sunflower oil
Lemon juice
Maldon salt
Fresh ground white pepper
You will also require one teatowel

Lightly oil a terrine tin and line it with clingfilm (roll up a teatowel and use it to help to push the clingfilm down).

Take six of the Parma ham slices and line the clingfilm with them, making sure a little overlaps the rim.

Top and tail the leeks so that they fit the terrine. Poach the leeks in boiling, salted water for five minutes. Remove the leeks with a slotted spoon and dump them into a bowl of cold water. After a further five minutes, drain the leeks. Wrap them gently in the teatowel and wring the excess moisture from the leeks, trying not to squeeze too hard, since this will remove too much juice.

Place two of the chicken breasts into a food processor and whizz until well broken down (this will take about three minutes). You'll have to stop once or twice to scrape the chicken from the sides of the bowl.

Once broken down, add the egg yolks and whizz again for about 90 seconds. Remove the bowl, complete with the chicken, egg and blade still in, and place it in the freezer for ten minutes. (Chilling the chicken down in this way makes it easier for the cream to be absorbed.)

Replace the bowl on the food processor and whizz again. Add the cream in a steady stream until you have a nice stiff mousse.

Now add the cooking salt and white pepper. Take a moment to taste as you season and try to end up being able to taste the salt and feel the heat of the pepper, but not so much that either dominate the mixture. (In other words, season to taste.)

Remove the fillets from the four remaining chicken breasts and then cut the remaining parts of the breasts into four long strips. This means you end up with 20 long strips of chicken.

Now heat up a frying pan until it's very hot. Meanwhile, season your chicken pieces with Maldon salt and fresh ground white pepper.

Add the sunflower oil to the pan and quickly stir fry the chicken pieces for no more than 45 seconds. The fillets should be starting to go opaque. Squeeze a little lemon juice over them, remove from the frying pan and leave to cool on a baking tray.

To assemble and cook the Terrine, pre-heat the oven to 180°C/350°F/Gas Mark 4. You should have to hand:

1) The chicken mousse
2) The leeks
3) The fried chicken strips
4) Terrine tin lined with clingfilm and Parma ham
5) 1 more piece of Parma ham

Place a tablespoon of the mousse into the bottom of the terrine tin and spread it out thinly. Place four leeks on top of the mousse, pressing them down. Season with a little salt, pepper and lemon juice. Place another tablespoon of mousse on top of this.

FOR THE OLIVE OIL AND CHERVIL SAUCE:

120 ml (4 fl oz) olive oil
1 tablespoon lemon juice
1 heaped tablespoon chervil, chopped

Now place eight chicken pieces onto the mousse.

Repeat this process twice (it's not dissimilar to constructing a lasagne) ending with a layer of leeks on the top and a final spread of the mousse. Place the remaining piece of Parma ham over the top of the terrine and fold over the Parma you used to line the tin, sealing the whole thing in.

Now pull the clingfilm out from the edges of the Terrine and stretch it over the top enclosing the terrine tin in clingfilm.

Finally, place the lid on the terrine, if it has one, or cover it with four thicknesses of foil.

Now place the terrine tin into a roasting tin and pour in hot water so that it comes halfway up the side of the terrine. Place this into the warmed oven, and cook for 45 minutes, after which it is necessary to test the terrine to see if it's ready.

To do this remove the terrine from the oven and remove the lid or tin foil and peel back the clingfilm. Plunge a skewer into the centre of the terrine and keep it there for ten seconds. Remove it and run the immersed part of the skewer over your lower lip. It should feel hot/warm/hot as you go from one end to the other. If it feels warm/cool/warm then the terrine needs further cooking. If this is the case give it another five minutes and test again.

When it's ready, remove it from the oven and allow it to cool down. Refrigerate the Terrine in the tin for 12 to 24 hours before serving.

When you are ready to serve, invert the terrine on a board and give it a tap and ease it out. Unwrap the clingfilm.

Place the terrine on a chopping board and using the sharpest knife (preferably serrated) cut it into 1 cm (½ in) slices.

To make the Olive Oil and Chervil Sauce, mix together all the ingredients with a wooden spoon. Simple.

Place one slice of the terrine on each serving plate. Pour round a little of the sauce. Serve.

WARM SALAD OF PIGEON WITH GREEN LENTILS, BACON AND AN OLIVE OIL DRESSING

This is the dish that turned me on to warm salads. It's completely barry (translated as great, fab, wonderful, Ed.) combination of flavours and textures. Try to get Puy lentils, as they have the best flavour (green or brown lentils would do though).

Keep the pigeon breasts nice and pink as they lose a lot of their texture and flavour if you overcook them. Keep any cooking juices to add to the salad – it's all extra flavour. Look for a good variation of colour and texture in the salad leaves. If you can't get celeriac, parsnip is a good substitute for the crunchy bits.

Pre-heat the oven to 220°C/425°F/Gas Mark 7.

Drain the lentils before placing them in a saucepan with just enough water to cover and cook them very slowly for eight to ten minutes until tender. Drain the lentils again and put them in a shallow dish. Keep them warm until required.

Heat the oil to 190°C (375°F) or until a bread cube turns golden in 20 seconds and rises. Deep fry the celeriac (or parsnip) slices until golden. Drain and leave them on a sheet of kitchen towel until required. Season with salt.

Season the pigeon breasts. Heat a frying pan until it's hot. Drop in the one tablespoon of sunflower oil and pan fry the pigeon breasts for approximately two minutes each side. Allow them to rest in the pan in a warm place for at least 10 minutes.

In the meantime, mix together the salad leaves, carrot, bacon and lentils in a large stainless steel bowl.

Slice the pigeon breasts thinly – about a dozen slices per breast (they should still be very pink inside) – and add them to the bowl of leaves.

Season with Maldon salt and white pepper. Pour over the oil and mix thoroughly until everything is

50 g (2 oz) Puy lentils, soaked overnight
150 g (5 oz) celeriac (or 1 parsnip), thinly sliced
4 wood pigeon breasts, skinned and boned
Sunflower oil for deep frying, plus 1 tablespoon
½ curly endive
½ lollo rosso
25 g (1 oz) rocket leaves
25 g (1 oz) mâche lettuce, all washed, dried and picked into rough 2.5-cm (1-in) pieces
1 small carrot, peeled and grated
2 rashers smoked back bacon, grilled to crispy and diced
1 large ripe plum Tomatoes Concasse (see page 171)
50 ml (2 fl oz) extra virgin olive oil
1 teaspoon lemon juice
Maldon salt
Fresh ground white pepper

SERVES FOUR

well coated. Pour over any pan juice from the pigeon. Squeeze in the lemon juice and mix again.

Place the bowl in a hot oven for 45 seconds, remove it and mix again.

To serve, divide the salad between four bowls and top them with the deep fried celeriac.

RISOTTO OF SMOKED HADDOCK

There are endless variations on the Risotto theme. This one uses a prime Scottish ingredient – smoked haddock. The skinless, boneless fillets are easy to use and, instead of the usual endless stirring normally required for risotto, I cheat by partially pre-cooking the Risotto, finishing it at the last minute. This is a fairly simple dish and so requires good ingredients – good stock, good Parmesan and Arborio rice are compulsory!

Do try to get undyed haddock.

500 ml (16 fl oz) Fish Stock (see page 161) (important: reserve 2 tablespoons for serving)
225 g (8 oz) smoked haddock, boneless and skinless
75 g (3 oz) unsalted butter
50 g (2 oz) onion, finely chopped
150 ml (¼ pint) white wine
165 g (6 oz) Arborio rice
25 g (1 oz) fresh Parmesan, grated (reserve 1 tablespoon for garnish)
2 tablespoons whipped cream
Pinch of saffron stamens, soaked in 1 tablespoon water

In a pan large enough to hold the fish fillet, first pour in the Fish Stock and heat until boiling. Then add the fillet, cover the pan and take it off the heat and leave to poach for ten minutes.

Remove the fish (it will be just slightly undercooked) and flake it by hand. Cover the fish and reserve it in fridge until needed. Keep the stock to one side.

In a medium-sized saucepan, melt the 50 g (2 oz) butter but don't let it brown. Add the onion and sweat it without browning for seven to eight minutes until soft. Add the rice and stir to coat it in the butter. Add the wine and saffron and increase the heat. Most of the wine will disappear quite quickly (about two or three minutes) and the mixture will become thick and sticky as you stir it with a wooden spoon.

Add the stock, bring to the boil and simmer for two minutes, stirring from time to time. Pour the mix into a sieve set over a bowl. Reserve the cooking liquid from the bowl in the fridge. Cool the rice on a tray, cover and store in the fridge until needed.

All of the above can be done up to 24 hours in advance, which just leaves the final cooking . . .

To serve, put the rice in a medium-sized saucepan and add the cooking liquid back, along with your reserved two tablespoons of fish stock. Put the rice on a medium heat, stirring from time to time. After about four or five minutes, the rice will start to thicken. Taste it to see if it's cooked (it should still have a bit of bite, but shouldn't be crunchy or soggy) and if it isn't carry on for another few minutes.

Add a little seasoning, then stir in the remaining butter, followed by most of the Parmesan and whipped cream. Lastly, add the flaked fish and fold it in. Taste again for seasoning and add a squeeze of lemon juice. Warm it through for approximately two minutes.

Divide the Risotto between four warmed shallow bowls and sprinkle on the remaining Parmesan. Scatter the chopped herbs and it's grub's up!

This should taste seriously good.

Lemon juice
1 tablespoon of mixed herbs (chives, parsley, dill), chopped
Maldon salt
Fresh ground white pepper

SERVES FOUR

PEARL BARLEY RISOTTO WITH CHANTERELLE MUSHROOMS

You don't get much more Scottish than this. Chanterelles appear in abundance all over Scotland between August and October and their characteristic yellow colour and wonderful perfume make them easy to recognise. Most, however, seem to be picked by professional mushroom pickers who export them. You can substitute any other wild mushrooms (or even button mushrooms) in this recipe, and if you use water or Vegetable Stock instead of Chicken Stock, it becomes a vegetarian starter.

The nutty flavour of the barley is a natural with the slightly exotic flavour of the mushrooms – another marriage made in Scotland!

50 ml (2 fl oz) olive oil

175 g (6 oz) pearl barley, washed and drained

1 small onion, finely chopped

½ garlic clove, minced

450 ml (¾ pint) Chicken Stock (see page 162) or water

2 tablespoons light Soy Sauce

150 ml (5 fl oz) red wine

225 g (8 oz) chanterelles (or other mushrooms)

50 g (2 oz) unsalted butter

1 tablespoon tarragon, chopped

Maldon salt

Fresh ground white pepper

SERVES FOUR

Heat a large frying pan until it's hot. Pour in the olive oil then add the barley and stir until it starts to turn golden – this will take about five minutes. Add the onion and garlic and continue frying until the barley starts to brown (about five to ten minutes). Don't let it burn. Add the Chicken Stock, Soy Sauce, red wine and seasoning. Reduce it until nearly all the liquid is gone.

Meanwhile, scrape clean the mushrooms (slicing any bigger ones to size) and heat another frying pan until it's hot. Add 25 g (1 oz) butter and the mushrooms. Stir fry until lightly coloured (this will take about four or five minutes). Season with salt and pepper.

Add the stir fried mushrooms to the barley and mix together. When the pan is nearly dry, remove it from heat and cover with tin foil with some holes pierced in it. Leave it in a warm place for 15 minutes.

At this stage, you could let the Risotto cool, reheating it for serving up to 24 hours later.

To serve, pop the pan back on the heat, add the tarragon and the remaining 25 g (1 oz) butter. Stir well until hot, taste for seasoning and serve.

Enjoy a real flavour of Scotland!

PART FOUR

FISH
MAIN COURSES

ROAST FILLET OF SALMON WITH NEW POTATOES, WILTED GREENS AND HOLLANDAISE

This simple dish perfectly illustrates the adage that good food doesn't have to be complicated. As with all simple dishes, you must obtain the best, freshest ingredients. Good quality farmed salmon (look for the tartan quality mark) is great – but this dish would be the perfect and most fitting end for a fine spring-run salmon. Seek out the best quality small, fresh new potatoes.

450 g (1 lb) small new potatoes, scrubbed (skin still on)
150 g (6 oz) melted butter
3 egg yolks, size 3
Lemon juice
4 tablespoons olive oil
4 × 150 g (5 oz) salmon fillets, skinless and boneless
50 g (2 oz) baby spinach leaves
25 g (1 oz) rocket leaves
25 g (1 oz) basil leaves
100 g (4 oz) mange tout, cut into thin strips lengthwise
Maldon salt
Fresh ground white pepper
1 tablespoon mint, chopped, to garnish

SERVES FOUR

First put the spuds in a pot of salted water (uncovered). Bring it to the boil then reduce the heat to a low simmer. They will take about 20 minutes to cook.

Meanwhile, prepare the Hollandaise. Place the egg yolks in a metal bowl big enough to fit over the pot of simmering spuds. Ensure that the melted butter is hot and ready for use in a few minutes.

Add one tablespoon of hot water to the yolks and place the bowl over the pot and get whisking. After four or five minutes, the yolks should be pale and thick. At this point, start adding the butter a tablespoon at a time, whisking each addition in. After you've added the first half of the butter, you may add it two tablespoons at a time until you've finished. (It is important not to allow the mixture to boil. If this happens, you'll be eating it on toast).

Once all of the butter has been incorporated, add a couple of pinches of salt, four turns of pepper and two teaspoons of lemon juice. Taste and check the seasoning and keep the Hollandaise warm whilst you prepare the salmon.

Have a metal tray near to hand before heating a large frying pan until it is hot. Add two tablespoons of olive oil to the pan and then put in the salmon fillets, prettiest side down. Fry them for three to four minutes until they are nicely browned. Turn them and do the same on the other side.

Remove the salmon to the metal tray, season it liberally with salt, pepper and lemon juice. Keep it warm whilst you prepare the greens.

To do this add two more tablespoons of olive oil to the frying pan and quickly bung in the greens. Stir fry them until they are wilted (it will take about two minutes), season them with a little salt, pepper and lemon juice. Remove them from the heat and keep them warm.

When the spuds are ready, drain and keep them warm.

To serve the meal, divide the potatoes between four warmed plates. Divide the greens equally over the potatoes and place the salmon fillets on top. Then spoon over the Hollandaise.

Lastly, sprinkle over some chopped mint and have your eatin' irons ready!

BAKED FILLET OF HALIBUT WITH CABBAGE, SMOKED BACON AND A TARRAGON CREAM SAUCE

Halibut is an absolutely topping fish – it has a beautiful texture and flavour, it's easy to fillet and the bones make good stock. No scales to get everywhere either! Obviously designed by experts, this fish is readily available during the summer months – but you have to be careful not to overcook it, since it can become dried out very easily, due to its low fat content.

It has sufficient flavour to partner the robust cabbage and bacon, which is all you really need for this dish. If you do want potatoes, however, I'd go for four portions of Rosti Potatoes (see page 128).

FOR THE HALIBUT:

4 × 150 g (5 oz) halibut fillets,
  skinless and boneless (steaks will
  do)
2 tablespoons dry white wine
1 small savoy cabbage
2 rashers smoked back bacon
1 tablespoon olive oil
50 g (2 oz) unsalted butter
Maldon salt
Fresh ground white pepper

Pre-heat the oven to 230°C/450°F/Gas Mark 8 for cooking the halibut later but first make the sauce. Melt the butter in a pan over a low to medium heat. Then sweat the shallots and mushrooms until they are soft. Add the bay leaf and tarragon stalks before increasing the heat to full and adding the white wine. Reduce it until it's nearly all gone.

Now add the Fish Stock and reduce it again until it's nearly all gone. Then add the cream. Bring it to the boil and pour the contents of the pan through a fine sieve, forcing it through with the bottom of a ladle into a small, clean saucepan.

Season it, adding a few drops of lemon juice to taste.

Now cook the cabbage and bacon. Heat a medium-sized saucepan until hot. Peel off the coarse, outer leaves of the cabbage and discard them. Give the centre part a good wash and then cut it lengthwise into quarters. Cut out the root part of each quarter, then finely shred the remaining cabbage with a sharp knife. Watch your fingers!

Cut the bacon into matchsticks. Pour the olive oil into the now very hot saucepan and stir fry the bacon matchsticks until crispy.

Add 25 g (1 oz) butter, then the cabbage and stir fry it for five to six minutes until the cabbage is tender. Season with salt and pepper and keep warm.

For the halibut, use 25 g (1 oz) butter to grease the base of a roasting tin. Place the fillets into the tin, season them with salt, pepper and lemon juice and dot the other 25 g (1 oz) of butter over the fish.

Now pour two tablespoons of wine into the pan to prevent the butter from burning.

Whack the roasting tin in to the hot oven. Set the timer for six minutes, then set up four warmed serving plates. Place four good-sized piles of the cabbage and bacon combo into the centre of each plate.

Chop the tarragon leaves and add it to the sauce before pouring it around each pile of cabbage and bacon.

If you are using Rosti, place an individual portion on top of each pile as well.

When the timer pings, remove the fish from the oven. It should be just cooked through and no more. Place a fillet in the centre of each plate – you can spoon over any juices left in the roasting tin for extra flavour – and hand them out to the lucky guests.

FOR THE TARRAGON CREAM SAUCE:

15 g (½ oz) unsalted butter
2 shallots, peeled and sliced
4 button mushrooms, finely sliced
1 bay leaf
3 sprigs tarragon, leaves picked (retain stalks)
300 ml (10 fl oz) Fish Stock (see page 161)
300 ml (10 fl oz) white wine
300 ml (10 fl oz) double cream
Lemon juice

SERVES FOUR

LOBSTER THERMIDOR

Lobster thermidor is both overlooked and underrated. The beauty of the dish is that it can all be prepared in advance and only needs a last minute grilling. Serve it with Potato Galette (see page 131) and salad.

2 × 750 g (1½ lb) live lobsters

FOR THE CHEESE SAUCE:
300 ml (10 fl oz) milk
15 g (½ oz) flour
15 g (½ oz) butter
50 g (2 oz) Parmesan, grated
1 egg yolk (size 3)
1 teaspoon Dijon mustard
Maldon salt
White pepper
Juice of 1 lemon
2 shallots, peeled and finely diced
75 ml (3 fl oz) white wine
6 basil leaves, chopped
4 portions Potato galette (see page 131)

SERVES FOUR

To prepare the lobsters: half fill a large pan with water and bring to the boil. Plunge the live lobsters into the pan, cover with the lid and cook for seven minutes. Remove the lobsters and place them into a bowl of iced water. Allow to cool for 15 minutes and remove them. Pull off the claws, crack them open and lift out the flesh and reserve it. Place the lobster body and tail on a board and cut in half lengthwise. Remove the meat and rinse out the empty shells and place them on a tea towel to drain. Dice all the lobster meat into 1-cm (½-in) pieces.

To make the cheese sauce: heat the milk until nearly boiling. Melt the butter in a saucepan and mix in the flour to make a roux. Cook the roux for two minutes and then pour on the boiling milk, mixing it well. As the sauce begins to thicken, use a small whisk and cook gently for 20 minutes, whisking frequently to prevent lumps. After 20 minutes, add 40 g (1½ oz) of the Parmesan and the mustard and season with the salt, pepper and lemon juice and continue cooking for two minutes, whisking continuously. Finally, beat in the egg yolk.

To serve: pre-heat the grill to the highest setting. Combine the shallots and wine in a saucepan and bring to the boil. Reduce the wine by three-quarters and add the lobster pieces to it. Add the basil and season with salt, pepper and lemon juice. Place the lobster shells on a grill tray and divide half of the cheese sauce between them. Then divide the lobster meat and top with the remaining cheese sauce. Sprinkle over the remaining Parmesan and place them under the grill until browned. Serve with the Potato Galette and a dressed salad.

BAKED FILLET OF COD WITH STEWED TOMATO, SPAGHETTI COURGETTE AND A PESTO BUTTER SAUCE

Cod is common and therefore taken very much for granted. Try this dish and you'll realise it shouldn't be. I love the combinations of colour, texture and flavour in this dish. If you want to serve potato with it, I'd go for Mash or Dauphinoise.

First pre-heat the oven to 230°C/450°F/Gas Mark 8 before preparing the vegetables.

Place the Concasse in a small pan with the olive oil, a little seasoning and three drops of lemon juice.

Wipe, top and tail the courgette and cut it into spaghetti-like strands. (I use a Mandolin grater, but you could grate it on a box grater or finely slice it with a sharp knife.) Place this in another small pan with 25 g (1 oz) butter, a little seasoning and half a teaspoon of lemon juice.

Reserve both pans until you are ready to serve.

Use 25 g (1 oz) butter to grease a roasting pan big enough to hold the cod fillets. Place the fillets in the tin and add 2 tablespoons of water to prevent the butter burning. Then season them with salt, pepper and lemon juice. Dot the remaining butter over the fillets.

Now warm through the Mash or the Dauphinoise potatoes. Also warm through the Nage Butter Sauce and place the spaghetti courgette on a high heat.

Bang the cod into the oven and set your timer for six minutes.

Stir the courgette and, once it starts to sizzle, cook for two minutes. Taste and check the seasoning. Then keep it warm.

Stir the Tomatoes Concasse, place them on a low heat and gently heat through without overcooking. It should stay firm and not go to pulp.

2 ripe plum Tomatoes Concasse (see page 171)
Lemon juice
1 large courgette
75 g (3 oz) unsalted butter
4 × 150 g (5 oz) cod fillets, skinless and boneless
150 ml (5 fl oz) Nage Butter Sauce (see page 164)
1 tablespoon olive oil
1 tablespoon chives, chopped
2 tablespoons Pesto (see page 167)
Maldon salt
Fresh ground white pepper
4 portions Mash (page 127) or Dauphinoise (page 126) potatoes

SERVES FOUR

Baked Fillet of Cod with Stewed
Tomato, Spaghetti Courgette and
a Pesto Butter Sauce (page 77).

When the timer goes off, remove the cod and allow to rest for two minutes. Lay out four warmed serving plates and place equal portions of courgettes to the side on each plate.

Add the Pesto to the butter sauce and whisk it in. Taste it and season. Spoon this over the courgette and place a fish fillet on top.

Neatly pile the warm tomato mix on top of each fillet and dust with the chives.

Place a dollop of your chosen potato dish at one side and serve.

ROAST FILLET OF MONKFISH WITH POTATO ROSTI, SPINACH AND RED WINE SAUCE

This dish is loosely based on steak and chips. The meaty texture of monkfish lends itself to this treatment. It has a huge head and a big, muscular tail (this is the bit you want). The head could be used to make stock, but personally I don't rate it much. Get your fishmonger to fillet and skin the tail for you and also to remove the centre bone, leaving you with two roughly triangular long strips of fillet. The sauce needs a light and fruity wine and I usually use a Beaujolais.

2 × 275 g (10 oz) fillets monkfish tail, skinned

3 tablespoons sunflower oil

4 Rosti Potatoes portions (see page 128)

225 g (8 oz) spinach leaves, washed and rough stalks and damaged pieces removed

Pre-heat the oven to 150°C/300°F/Gas Mark 2.

Prepare the Rosti and leave it to rest (see page 128).

To make the sauce, pour the wine into a medium-sized stainless steel saucepan and place it over a high heat, reducing it until it's nearly gone. Add the fish stock and reduce it by two thirds.

Add the diced, cold butter and shake the pan over the heat until all the butter has melted and the sauce is dark and glossy. Keep it warm.

Now roast the monkfish. First heat a frying pan until it's very hot. Season the monkfish fillets all over with salt and fresh ground white pepper. Add the sunflower oil to the roasting hot pan and lightly fry the fish fillets for two to four minutes on each of their three sides, depending on their thickness, then lift the pan to a warm place and leave the fish to relax for 10 minutes.

Place the Rosti on a tray and put it into the low oven to heat it through.

Heat a large pan until it's hot, add one teaspoon of olive oil, then dump in the spinach and stir fry it until it's wilted. (This will take about two minutes.) Season with the salt, pepper and lemon juice.

Have four warm plates ready and divide the spinach between them, placing it in the centre. Position a warmed Rosti on top of the spinach portions.

Remove the fillets from the pan and dribble a few drops of lemon juice over them. Carve each fillet into six slices and arrange three slices of monk atop each Rosti.

Strain any pan juices into the sauce and adjust seasoning before spooning it around the fish and serving.

1 tablespoon olive oil (for cooking
  the spinach)
Maldon salt
Fresh ground white pepper
Lemon juice

FOR THE SAUCE:

300 ml (10 fl oz) Beaujolais
450 ml (15 fl oz) Fish Stock (see
  page 000)
75 g (3 oz) unsalted butter, cold
  and diced
Lemon juice
Maldon salt
Fresh ground white pepper

SERVES FOUR

LEFT: Steamed Fillet of Brill on a
Bed of Celery with a Grain
Mustard Sauce (page 84).
RIGHT: Seared Fillet of Salmon
with an Avocado Salsa and
Oriental Sauce Vierge (page 20).

STEAMED FILLET OF BRILL ON A BED OF CELERY WITH A GRAIN MUSTARD SAUCE

I use an old, battered aluminium steamer which I bought in Habitat years ago. Bamboo Chinese steamers work very well, but you could use anything which holds water, can fit a rack to put the fish on and has a lid to hold in the steam. Steaming helps keep the fish flesh nice and white looking and is, as we all know, the healthier option.

Brill is a cheaper version of turbot, just as tasty (but not quite as meaty) and cheaper at about two thirds of the price. As usual, get your fishmonger to do the dirty work and give you the fillets.

This eats well with Fondant (see page 130) or Galette (see page 131) Potatoes.

6 sticks celery, peeled

2 tablespoons olive oil

85 ml (3 fl oz) water

4 × 150 g (5 oz) fillets of brill

150 ml (5 fl oz) Nage Butter Sauce (see page 164)

2 teaspoons best quality grain mustard

1 tablespoon chopped fresh flat leaf parsley

Maldon salt

Fresh ground white pepper

Lemon juice

SERVES FOUR

Prepare four portions of Fondant Potatoes (see page 130) or Galette Potatoes (see page 131) and keep them warm until they are needed.

Prepare the celery by cutting the stalks into batons 4 cm × 5 mm × 5 mm (1½ × ¼ × ¼ in) in size and fry them quickly in the olive oil. Season it with salt, pepper and lemon juice and pour over the water. Reduce on a medium heat until nearly all the liquid has gone and the celery is cooked. Keep it warm until it's needed.

Place the brill in a steamer, season and steam until just cooked. This will take about three or four minutes.

Warm through the Nage Butter Sauce.

Lay out four warm serving plates and divide the celery between them. Place a brill fillet half over each celery pile.

Remove the Nage Butter Sauce from the heat and add the mustard to it. Check for seasoning and spoon the sauce and mustard mix over the brill and celery.

Lay whichever potato garnish you've prepared next to the fish, scatter over the parsley and amaze your guests with this deeply wonderful dish.

Fillet of cod with spring onion mash and a caviar butter sauce

I've said it before, but cod deserves more of the limelight and this dish is an excellent way of showing off its star qualities. This is a very posh fish pie, but if you don't feel extravagant, skip the caviare and double the amount of chives in the sauce.

Pre-heat the oven to 230°C/450°F/Gas Mark 8.

Boil the potatoes in salted water then simmer for about 20–30 minutes until just tender. Drain and dry out in the pre-heated oven for a further five minutes.

Take out the dried potatoes and mash them. Add the melted butter, olive oil, spring onions and seasoning. Beat everything in with a wooden spoon until nice and fluffy and place them in a dish. Cover it with foil and keep warm.

Heat and season the Nage Butter Sauce. Then place a large pan on the stove and heat until hot for the spinach.

Place the cod fillets on a well-buttered baking dish. Season them and pour in two tablespoons of water to prevent the butter from burning.

Dot the top of the cod with pinch-sized pieces of butter and squeeze over a little lemon juice. Season with crushed salt and pepper.

Put the cod into the oven for six minutes until it is just cooked (they should look translucent, not cracked).

While the cod is cooking, drop the olive oil into the pre-heated pan, add the spinach and stir fry it. Season it with salt, pepper and lemon juice. Remove the cod and allow to rest for two minutes.

Take the warmed Nage Butter Sauce from the heat and stir in the caviar, if you are using it, and the chives at the last minute.

---

2 large baking potatoes, total weight 675 g (1½ lb), peeled and quartered

50 g (2 oz) melted butter

25 ml (1 fl oz) olive oil

3 spring onions, finely sliced

150 ml (5 fl oz) Nage Butter Sauce (see page 164)

4 × 150 g (5 oz) cod fillets, skinned and boned

Lemon juice

175 g (6 oz) young tender spinach leaves

1 teaspoon Sevruga caviar (optional)

2 teaspoons chopped chives (or 4 teaspoons if not using caviar)

Maldon salt

Fresh ground white pepper

SERVES FOUR

To serve, lay out four warmed serving plates, placing a little spinach on each. Add a scoop of potato on top, flattening it slightly. Place a cod fillet on top of each one and spoon on your caviar butter sauce.

I cannot begin to express my unalloyed enthusiasm for this dish. Get serving.

SEARED FILLET OF JOHN DORY ON A BED OF POTATO AND ONIONS WITH A CAPER, OLIVE, TOMATO AND BASIL SAUCE

This is a dish of robust flavours and makes good use of John Dory (see the recipe on page 47 for another good one). It is not a dish for the faint hearted.

4 × 150 g (5 oz) portions Boulangère Potatoes (see page 129)

120 ml (4 fl oz) Mediterranean Sauce Vierge (see page 176)

2 portions of Tomatoes Concasse (see page 171)

12 black olives, stoned and quartered

20 dry salted capers, rinsed

2 tablespoons olive oil

4 × 150 g (5 oz) fillets John Dory, skinned and boned

12 leaves basil, finely diced

Maldon salt

Fresh ground white pepper

Lemon juice

SERVES FOUR

Pre-heat the oven to 180°C/350°F/Gas Mark 4.

Place the four Boulangère portions onto a baking tray and put it into the oven. Warm through the Mediterranean Sauce Vierge and add the olives and capers. Keep it warm.

Heat a frying pan until it's hot, add the olive oil and fry the John Dory fillets for three minutes on one side only.

Lift them off onto a warmed plate, turning the seared side up, and season them with the salt, pepper and lemon juice. Keep them warm.

Add the tomato and basil to the sauce. Stir and taste.

To serve, lay out four warm serving plates. Take the potato from the oven and place a portion into the centre of each plate. Place a Dory fillet on each pile of potato and spoon the sauce over and around. Give each serving its fair share of olives, capers and tomatoes.

Now serve.

PART FIVE

POULTRY
AND DUCK
MAIN COURSES

TARRAGON CHICKEN

To get the best from this classic French dish takes a little understanding. It was one of the first dishes I cooked at home, using stock cubes, dried herbs and frozen chicken and even then, it tasted pretty good. However, the recipe has evolved and developed over the years and you should taste it now!

My advice is to use chicken legs, (since chicken breasts are virtually fat free and will dry out during the long cooking) preferably from a maize- or corn-fed chicken. To split the chicken legs: lay the joint on a board and place a knife in the centre of the joint. If you have the knife in the right position, the two will spring up when you press the knife down and they will separate quite easily.

My favourite accompaniment with this is fresh pasta, fresh bread and salad. Any combination of potato and vegetable, however, is just grand.

6 chicken legs (skin on and split into thigh and drumstick)

2 tablespoons sunflower oil for frying

50 g (2 oz) unsalted butter

I large Spanish onion, peeled and sliced

I garlic clove, crushed

15 g (1 oz) tarragon leaves, (reserve stalks)

165 g (6 oz) button mushrooms, sliced in half

300 ml (10 fl oz) white wine

600 ml (20 fl oz) Chicken Stock (see page 162)

Few drops of lemon juice

Maldon salt

Fresh ground white pepper

SERVES SIX

Heat a large frying pan until hot. Then add two tablespoons of sunflower oil. Season the chicken joints with the salt and pepper and fry them four at a time until golden brown.

Meanwhile, heat a large saucepan or casserole until it is hot. Add the butter, then the onions, garlic and tarragon stalks. Stir and cook for about five to ten minutes until they start to colour. Add the white wine and reduce the volume by about three quarters.

Add the sautéed chicken legs, fling in the mushrooms and pour in the stock. Pour over just enough water to cover the chicken and add a few drops of lemon juice. Bring it to the boil and immediately lower the heat, skimming off any fat or impurities. Simmer very gently with a lid on for one hour, skimming occasionally.

Remove the lid and inspect the chicken. If it's nearly falling off the bone, it's done. Remove it with a slotted spoon and put it aside. Now increase the heat and reduce the cooking liquor by half. Take the skin off the chicken and discard. You can also take the chicken off the bone if you like, but I usually don't bother. Once reduced, remove the tarragon stalks. Put the chicken back in. Then chop the tarragon leaves and fling them into the casserole.

Check seasoning and you're ready to serve, although personally I'd just plonk the casserole on the table and let the guests help themselves.

For a 'cheat' version of this recipe, see below.

'CHEATTIE' TARRAGON CHICKEN

I adore chicken with tarragon. It's a marriage made in Scotland! But you could also try chervil, which has a milder flavour. In this recipe, I use chicken breast, so the entire cooking time is 20 minutes. Serve with new potatoes and a few lightly fried courgettes or other green vegetables.

Heat a large frying pan until it's hot. Season the chicken breasts, add the olive oil and then the butter to the pan and whack in the chicken breasts. Cook for two to three minutes on each side until nicely browned.

Add the onion, mushrooms and garlic and stir well, chasing them round the pan to absorb the juices and prevent them from burning. Once the onion has started to soften, add the wine, which should boil off fairly quickly, then add the Stock and reduce it over a high heat. Turn the chicken breasts a couple of times to ensure they cook evenly.

When the stock has become very thick, add the cream and the tarragon and boil again. Check the seasoning and add a few drops of lemon juice. Keep it warm until you are ready to serve. (If you are keeping it for any length of time don't add the tarragon. Cover it with a butter wrapper to prevent the skin from drying out and leave it to cool. When reheating, add two tablespoons of water and the tarragon first.)

To serve, lay out four warm plates, placing a chicken breast on each one and spoon the sauce over. Arrange the suggested vegetables and serve.

4 chicken breast fillets, skinless
1 tablespoon olive oil
50 g (2 oz) unsalted butter
1 medium onion, diced
120 g (4 oz) button mushrooms, cut in halves
1 garlic clove, crushed
150 ml (5 fl oz) white wine
300 ml (10 fl oz) Chicken Stock (see page 162). Alternatively, a chicken stock cube would suffice here.
150 ml (5 fl oz) double cream
15 g (½ oz) tarragon leaves
Maldon salt
Fresh ground white pepper
Lemon juice

SERVES FOUR

Roast Breast of Guinea Fowl
with Seared Vegetables and a
Tapenade Sauce (page 92).

ROAST BREAST OF GUINEA FOWL WITH SEARED VEGETABLES AND A TAPENADE SAUCE

A lot of people are suspicious of guinea fowl because it's unfamiliar. They needn't be – it's similar to chicken, only tastier, with a faint, gamey tang and real flavour. If you get a chance to get some, go for it.

Tapenade is currently in vogue but none the worse for that. I would go for Mashed Potatoes or Dauphinoise with this (see pages 127 and 126 respectively), or sautéed new potatoes.

1 Roasted Red Pepper (see page 174)
1 small aubergine
1–2 teaspoons refined salt
2 medium courgettes
50 g (2 oz) unsalted butter
2 shallots, thinly sliced
4 button mushrooms
1 bay leaf
1 sprig thyme
300 ml (10 fl oz) Chicken Stock (see page 162)
200 ml (7 fl oz) double cream
1–2 tablespoons Tapenade (see page 168)
4 guinea fowl breasts, skin on
Sunflower oil
Olive oil
300 ml (10 fl oz) red wine
Maldon salt
Fresh ground white pepper
Lemon juice

SERVES FOUR

Pre-heat the oven to 230°C/450°F/Gas Mark 8.

Start with the vegetables and have the red pepper standing by. Wipe, top and tail the aubergine and cut it into eight slices. Lightly salt these with the refined salt. Leave them to drain for 15 minutes, then wash and leave them to drain again in a sieve.

Top, tail and wipe the courgettes and, cutting downwards, cut into four 45 degree angled slices each.

Set the vegetables aside until they are needed.

To make the sauce, heat a medium-sized saucepan to a medium temperature. Add the butter and, when it sizzles, add the shallots, mushrooms, bay leaf and thyme. Gently fry them until golden, add the wine and reduce it until nearly dry. Add the stock and reduce it by two-thirds. Then add the cream and the Tapenade. (If you really like the flavour, add two tablespoons.)

Bring it to the boil, then force the sauce through a fine sieve into a small clean saucepan. Keep it warm.

Now cook the guinea fowl. Heat a large frying pan until hot. Season the breasts with salt and pepper.

Add one tablespoon of olive oil to the hot frying pan followed by the rest of the butter. When the butter starts to brown, add the guinea fowl breasts, skin side up, and cook them for two minutes.

Turn over, skin side down, and cook for a further three to four minutes until the skin is dark brown.

Squeeze in one teaspoon lemon juice and place the pan in the oven for two minutes. Remove and turn the guinea fowl to skin side up and allow it to rest in a warm place for at least 10 minutes but no more than 30 minutes.

Heat a large frying pan until hot and, using a clean teatowel, pat dry the aubergine slices. Pour a 3 mm (⅛ inch) depth of oil into the frying pan and carefully add the aubergine slices (a pair of metal tongs will come in handy here because it may spit). Fry them until nearly black, turn them over and fry the other side. Place the aubergine on a warm metal tray and keep warm. Tip out the oil from the frying pan and replace it with two tablespoons of fresh olive oil. Add the courgette cut faces down and cook it until the cut side is nicely browned. This should take two to three minutes.

Season with Maldon salt and four turns of pepper. Squeeze over a teaspoon of lemon juice and stir everything with a wooden spoon until well coated.

Lift the courgette out and add it onto the tray with the aubergine.

Now fling the pepper quarters into the pan and quickly stir fry them. Season them with salt, pepper and lemon juice, cook for a further minute and add them to the tray. Keep the vegetables warm.

To serve, lay out four warmed serving plates and divide the seared vegetables between them. Pop the pan with the guinea fowl back into the hot oven for 90 seconds to reheat it.

Place your chosen potato garnish next to the vegetables. Check that the sauce is hot and taste it for seasoning (the Tapenade is quite salty, so it won't need much more added). Spoon the sauce around the vegetables and spuds.

Remove the frying pan from the oven and cut each guinea fowl breast into three pieces and place them, skin side up, next to the vegetables. Skim any fat from the pan juices and drizzle the juices over each breast. Now serve, pronto.

Roast Breast of Mallard with a
Confit of Root Vegetables and a
Mushroom and Tarragon Sauce
(page 96).

ROAST BREAST OF MALLARD WITH A CONFIT OF ROOT VEGETABLES AND A MUSHROOM AND TARRAGON SAUCE

Mallard are in season from September to January. However, I usually wait until about the end of October when the birds have a bit more weight on them. They are at their best and cheapest around Christmas, and faced with a choice between mallard and turkey . . .

One breast weighs about 175 g (6 oz) and is a perfect-sized portion. The meat is dark and rich, but not too gamey. The only drawback is that mallard fly most of the time, unlike reared ducks, and so have small, underdeveloped legs. I just bung these in with the carcasses to make seriously good game stock (just follow the method for Chicken Stock on page 162).

Also, get your butcher to prepare your birds for you if you're unsure. Fondant or Galette Potatoes are best with this dish (see pages 130 and 131 respectively).

2 mallard duck, breasts removed and carcasses used to make stock. (Or use Chicken Stock, page 162)

FOR THE VEGETABLE CONFIT:
2 tablespoons sunflower oil
¼ turnip (English swede), peeled and cut into eight slices
2 medium carrots, peeled and cut into eight pieces
4 sticks of celery, cut into 5-cm (2-in) lengths
2 tablespoons duck fat (or 1 tablespoon Sunflower oil and 25 g (1 oz) butter, combined)
Water

Pre-heat the oven to 230°C/450°F/Gas Mark 8.

To make the sauce, put the port and the red wine in a small saucepan and reduce the volume until it's nearly gone. Add the duck (or chicken) stock and reduce it by half. Add the butter and shake the pan until the butter dissolves but don't boil it. Keep it warm.

For the Confit of Root Vegetables, heat a large cast or black iron frying pan which is suitable for oven use. When it's hot, add the duckfat (or a sunflower and butter alternative). Then add the turnip, carrot and celery and fry for about five or six minutes until well coloured, turning the vegetables at least once. Season with salt and pepper then pour on enough cold water to just cover the vegetables and no more. Bring it to the boil and reduce it by two thirds, then bang the pan into the hot oven and cook for about 12 minutes. By this time, the rest of the water will have been absorbed and the vegetables will be just tender. They will keep warm in a cool oven for up to one hour.

For the mushrooms, scrape away any dirt and trim off any roots or soft bits before slicing them into even pieces. Heat a frying pan, add 15 g (½ oz) butter and then fling in the mushrooms. Lightly fry for four to five minutes until nicely browned.

If the mushrooms are wet and start to release a lot of liquid (looking like they're stewing), tip the contents of the frying pan into a sieve and shake out all the moisture. Wipe the pan, heat it again, add a further 15 g (½ oz) butter, add the mushrooms once more and carry on frying! Season with salt and pepper and a few drops of lemon juice. Keep them warm.

To cook the mallard, you need to heat a large frying pan until hot. Add the sunflower oil and heat it until smoking. Season the mallard breasts with salt and pepper then add them to the pan, skin side up.

Cook for two minutes, then turn skin side down and cook for a further 5–10 minutes depending on how thick the breast is and how pink you like your duck. Turn skin side up once more, remove the pan from heat and allow the mallard breasts to relax in the pan in a warm place for at least 10 and up to 30 minutes.

To serve, warm the sauce through, add the mushrooms. Chop and add the tarragon. Taste to check the seasoning and stir in the cassis before popping the mallard back into the oven for 90 seconds.

Lay out four warmed plates and divide the Vegetable Confit between them in four neat piles. Place the potato garnish next to the vegetables. Carve each breast into three and place next to the potato and vegetables. Spoon the sauce and the mushrooms over and serve.

Maldon salt
Fresh ground white pepper

FOR THE SAUCE:

150 ml (5 fl oz) ruby port
150 ml (5 fl oz) red wine
450 ml (15 fl oz) Duck or Chicken
  Stock (see page 162)
25 g (1 oz) cold unsalted butter,
  diced

FOR THE MUSHROOMS:

175 g (6 oz) mixed wild mushrooms
  (choose from: chantarelle, cep,
  pied mouton, blewit, trompette,
  shitake, pleurotte. If unobtainable,
  then ordinary brown cap will do.)
1 tablespoon chopped fresh
  tarragon
15 g (½ oz) unsalted butter
1 teaspoon cassis

FOR THE POTATO GARNISH:

4 portions Galette (see page 131) or
  Fondant (see page 130) Potatoes

SERVES FOUR

SEARED BREAST OF CHICKEN WITH BUTTER BEANS, TOMATO, CHILLI AND GARLIC

This is an easy peasy dish with all the work being done beforehand. It makes a perfect lunch served with some dressed salad leaves.

225 g (8 oz) dried butter beans
1 bay leaf
1 sprig thyme
2 garlic cloves, crushed
White pepper
Maldon salt
50 ml (2 fl oz) olive oil
1 small onion, finely chopped
1 red chilli, finely diced
1 × 225 g (8 oz) tin of chopped
    tomatoes
150 ml (5 fl oz) red wine
300 ml (10 fl oz) Chicken stock (see
    page 162)
4 × 150–175 g (5–6 oz) chicken
    breasts, skinned
25 ml (1 fl oz) sunflower oil
25 g (1 oz) butter
1 tablespoon chopped chives

SERVES FOUR

Soak the butter beans in cold water for 12 hours. Drain them and place in a clean saucepan and add 1 litre (2 pints) of cold water, the bay leaf, sprig of thyme, a crushed garlic clove, six turns of pepper. Bring them to the boil, reduce to simmer and continue cooking for 45–60 minutes, until they are tender. Add one heaped teaspoon of salt after 30 minutes.

To make the sauce: heat a large frying pan until warm, add the olive oil, onion, remaining garlic and the chilli and fry gently until golden. Increase the heat and add the tomatoes and red wine and reduce until the pan is nearly dry. Add the stock and reduce until the sauce starts to thicken.

When the beans are ready, drain them, picking out the bay, thyme and garlic, and add them to the sauce. Bring the sauce and beans back to the boil, season and allow them to cool.

Pre-heat the oven to 230°C/450°F/Gas Mark 8. Heat a large, all-metal frying pan until hot. Season the chicken breasts. Add the sunflower oil and butter to the pan and when the butter foams, add the breasts and fry for three minutes on each side. Pop the pan into the oven and cook for two minutes. Remove the pan and allow the breasts to relax for ten minutes.

To serve: warm through the beans and sauce and add the chopped chives. Reheat the chicken in the oven for 1½ minutes. Divide the beans and sauce between four shallow bowls, carve each chicken breast into slices and place in the centre of the bowls, and serve.

PART SIX

GAME
MAIN COURSES

ROAST BREAST OF PIGEON WITH CABBAGE, BACON AND A GAME SAUCE

Tender, tasty, lean and cheap – pigeon deserves more exposure! Here, it partners well with savoy cabbage flavoured with smoked bacon, all pulled together with a gamey sauce.

If you're buying whole pigeons and removing the breasts yourself, you can use the carcasses to make stock (use the same method as for Chicken Stock, page 162) – it's brilliant! If you want to remove the breasts yourself but aren't sure how to do it, ask your butcher to do one for you first – it's easy.

This is great with Mashed Potatoes, but any potato dish would do.

4 oven-ready woodpigeons, the 8
  breasts removed and skinned
1 small savoy cabbage
2 rashers smoked bacon
2 tablespoons sunflower oil
50 g (2 oz) unsalted butter
Maldon salt
Fresh ground white pepper
Cooking salt

FOR THE SAUCE:

25 g (I oz) unsalted butter
3 shallots, finely sliced
6 button mushrooms, sliced
I clove garlic, crushed
I bay leaf
I sprig thyme
6 white peppercorns, crushed
I teaspoon redcurrant jelly
125 ml (4¼ fl oz) red wine vinegar
120 ml (4 fl oz) port
175 ml (6 fl oz) Pigeon or Chicken
  Stock (see page 162)
50 ml (2 fl oz) double cream

Pre-heat the oven to 230°C/450°F/Gas Mark 8.

Make the Sauce first by heating a medium-sized saucepan until it's hot. Add 25 g (1 oz) of butter and the shallots. Then add the mushrooms, garlic, bay leaf, thyme and crushed white peppercorns.

Gently fry for five to ten minutes until golden brown. Add the redcurrant jelly and allow it to melt and be absorbed.

Pour in the red wine vinegar, followed by the port and boil it until the pan is dry. Then add the stock and reduce it by two thirds.

Add the cream, bring it back to the boil and pass it through a fine sieve into a small, clean pan. Check the seasoning and keep it warm until ready.

If you are making this Sauce the day before, allow it to cool, then cover it and store it in the fridge until needed.

Take the cabbage and remove the coarse outer leaves and discard them. Wash the heart of the cabbage in cold water. Quarter it, cut out the stem and, using a sharp knife, finely shred the cabbage. Start to heat a large saucepan.

Cut the bacon into matchsticks, add two tablespoons of sunflower oil to the hot pan and chuck in the bacon. Give it a bit of a stir until the bacon is nice and crispy. Add 25 g (1 oz) of butter, followed by the cabbage, stir fry it for five to seven minutes until it's soft and tender, then remove from the heat and keep warm.

To cook the pigeon, heat a large frying pan until very hot. Season the pigeon breasts on both sides with cooking salt and fresh ground white pepper.

Add two tablespoons of sunflower oil to the hot pan, then the pigeon breasts, with what was the skin side down until you skinned them. Fling in the remaining 25 g (1 oz) of butter and allow it to foam and brown.

After two minutes, turn the breasts over to cook for one minute on the other side. Remove the frying pan from the heat and leave it for ten minutes in a warm place to relax the meat.

To serve, heat through the Mashed Potatoes and warm the sauce. Check the cabbage is warm. Lay out four warmed serving plates.

Pour the juice and oil from the pigeon pan into the cabbage mixture and stir it well. Check the seasoning. It shouldn't need any salt but may take three to four turns of fresh ground white pepper.

Pop the pigeon into the hot oven for 60 seconds to reheat.

Place a bed of the cabbage and bacon onto each plate and place a scoop of the Mash next to that.

Remove the pigeon from the oven and cut each breast in half. Fan the two halved breasts (*i.e.* four pieces of pigeon) out on each bed of cabbage, spoon over the game sauce and serve.

FOR THE POTATO GARNISH:
Prepared Mashed Potatoes (see page 127)

SERVES FOUR

Roast Breast of pigeon with
Cabbage, Bacon and a Game
Sauce (page 100).

ROAST SADDLE OF ROE DEER WITH BRAISED RED CABBAGE AND A GAME AND CHOCOLATE SAUCE

Roe are the smallest and consequently the most tender deer, and the saddle is, in turn, the deer's most tender part. They are in season from the beginning of April until the end of October.

It's not really worth making a smaller quantity of the red cabbage. It does freeze well and is delicious with most game animals or birds. The chocolate may seem an odd flavour for a savoury sauce, but bitter chocolate (with 60% or more cocoa solids) complements gamey flavours well, and also gives the sauce a dark gloss.

Your butcher should prepare the saddle for you, giving you the two loins and the meaty trimmings. Get him to chop the rib bones into 2.5 cm (1 in) pieces.

This is a bit of a 'star' dish and requires some pre-planning. Consequently, your starter and pudding should be simple. To accompany, I would serve Dauphinoise Potatoes.

1 small roe saddle (1.5 kg/3½ lbs)
1 tablespoon Duck Fat (see page 165) or ½ tablespoon butter and ½ sunflower oil, mixed
Maldon salt
Fresh ground white pepper

FOR THE BRAISED CABBAGE:
1 red cabbage
50 g (2 oz) redcurrant jelly
50 ml (2 fl oz) sherry vinegar
Zest and juice of 1 orange
120 ml (4 fl oz) port
1 bottle red wine
85 g (3 oz) raisins

Pre-heat the oven to 230°C/450°F/Gas Mark 8.

To make ten portions of red cabbage, remove the coarse outer leaves. Quarter it and cut out and bin the root. Finely slice the cabbage using a sharp knife. Heat a large pan and add 50 g (2 oz) of the butter. When it sizzles, add the cabbage and stir it to coat. Add the redcurrant jelly and allow it to melt. Add the vinegar, orange, port, half of the red wine and some seasoning.

Bring it to the boil, reduce to a simmer and cook it until the liquid has reduced to a syrup and the cabbage is tender. This should take one hour.

Leave it to cool for 1 hour, add the raisins and cook for a further ½ hour. When it's ready, check and adjust the seasoning.

For the Sauce, roast the chopped bones in hot oven for 20 minutes until nicely browned. Drain off any fat and put to one side.

Heat a saucepan (large enough to hold the bones) and add 25 g (1 oz) of butter. Add the meaty trimmings and fry until browned. Now add the shallots, mushrooms, bay, thyme, peppercorns and fry everything until golden.

Add the remaining half of the red wine and reduce it until it's nearly gone. Add the bones and the two stocks (and a little water, if necessary, to ensure the bones are covered) and simmer for approximately one hour until well flavoured.

Strain off the sauce, allow it to stand for a few minutes. Spoon off any fat, put it into a clean pot and reduce it until thickened. You will be left with about 300 ml (10 fl oz) of Sauce.

For the meat, when you are nearly ready to serve, heat a frying pan until it's hot. Season the roe loins with salt and pepper (you may have to cut them in half to fit the pan). Add the duckfat or butter and sunflower oil combination to the pan. Then add the loins and lightly fry each side for three to four minutes respectively until well browned.

Remove the pan to a warm place to relax the meat for at least ten minutes (but no more than 30). Warm through four large spoonfuls of the cabbage in a small saucepan and warm through the Sauce. Pour any juices from the relaxing meat into the cabbage, then reheat the meat in the oven for 90 seconds. Have the Dauphinoise Potatoes ready.

Place a spoonful of cabbage on each of four warmed serving plates, placing the potato alongside. Carve the meat into approximately 24 slices and lay six slices on each pile of cabbage. Add the grated chocolate to the heated sauce and whisk it. Check and adjust the seasoning before spooning it over the meat.

FOR THE SAUCE:

Rib bones, chopped
Meaty trimmings
25 g (1 oz) unsalted butter
4 shallots, peeled and finely sliced
60 g (2 oz) button mushrooms, thinly sliced
1 bay leaf
1 sprig thyme
6 white peppercorns, crushed
600 ml (20 fl oz) Chicken Stock (see page 162)
300 ml (10 fl oz) Beef Stock (see page 163)
10 g (¼ oz) bitter chocolate, grated

FOR THE POTATO GARNISH:

4 portions Dauphinoise Potatoes (see page 126)

SERVES FOUR

TRADITIONAL ROAST GROUSE

The best way to appreciate the unique flavour of grouse is to serve it simply without sauces and fancy garnishes — a perfectly cooked bird accompanied by bread sauce and game gravy is all that is required.

4 × young grouse, oven-ready
4 slices of bread
300 ml (10 fl oz) red wine
1 tablespoon Cassis
600 ml (1 pint) game stock
300 ml (10 fl oz) milk
165 g (6½ oz) unsalted butter
75 ml (3 fl oz) Clarified butter (see page 175)
2 tablespoons sunflower oil
Breadcrumbs (see page 173)
½ an onion, studded with 3 cloves
1 garlic clove, crushed
5 bay leaves
12 juniper berries
5 sprigs of thyme
Maldon salt
White pepper
Watercress

SERVES FOUR

Firstly, make a milk infusion for the bread sauce. In a pan add the onion, bay leaf, thyme, crushed garlic and 50 g (2 oz) of the butter to the milk and bring it to the boil. Simmer the milk for five minutes and allow it to stand to infuse.

To prepare the birds: place three juniper berries, one sprig of thyme and one bay leaf into each cavity, smear the outside of each bird with 25 g (1 oz) of butter and place them in the fridge until you are ready to cook them.

Next, make some large croûtons using a scone cutter to stamp out four 6-cm (2½-in) discs of bread. Heat the Clarified butter in a pan and gently shallow-fry the discs until golden. Drain them on kitchen paper and reserve them until they are needed for serving.

To make the game gravy: combine the red wine, Cassis and game stock in a saucepan and reduce the liquid by boiling rapidly until it starts to thicken. Whisk in 15 g (½ oz) butter, season and keep warm until ready to serve.

Pre-heat the oven to 230°C/450°F/Gas Mark 8.

Heat a 30-cm (12-in) black iron frying pan until it is very hot. Add two tablespoons of sunflower oil and place the seasoned birds in the pan breast side down and cook for two minutes. Turn them onto the other side and seas for a further two minutes — both breasts should now be nicely browned. Then turn them onto their undersides and place the pan in the oven and cook for eight minutes. Remove them from the oven and allow the pan to stand in a warm place for at least ten minutes to allow the meat to relax.

Finish the bread sauce by straining the infused milk into a clean saucepan. Add the breadcrumbs and whisk over a medium heat for two to three minutes until thickened. Season well with Maldon salt and freshly ground white pepper.

Warm both the croûtons and the game sauce in the oven and check the seasoning of the sauce.

To serve: have four plates warmed and ready and place a croûton on each one. Then sit a grouse on top of the croûton and fill the cavity with a bunch of watercress. Dollop some bread sauce beside the bird and pour over a quarter of the game sauce. Repeat with the remaining three grouse and serve with a bowl of rowan jelly and plain boiled potatoes.

PAN-FRIED PHEASANT BREAST WITH CARAMELISED APPLES, CHESTNUTS AND A CIDER AND CHERVIL SAUCE

Pheasant comes into season in October, but it's best waiting until December, since the price falls dramatically (and the birds are nice and plump!). The main problem with cooking pheasant is that (like pigeon) it has a very low fat content and is prone to becoming dry, especially if overcooked.

This dish has a nice creamy sauce which moistens the pheasant and it's probably what I'll be having for Christmas dinner. I use vacuum-packed chestnuts – not quite as good as the real thing, but a hell of a lot easier.

I like to eat this with roast potatoes.

2 Granny Smith apples

4 pheasant breasts, skinned

50 g (2 oz) unsalted butter

16 small button mushrooms

300 ml (10 fl oz) dry cider

300 ml (10 fl oz) Chicken Stock
  (see page 162)

300 ml (10 fl oz) double cream

16 chestnuts, vacuum-packed

2 tablespoons chervil, roughly
  chopped

1 teaspoon icing sugar

Lemon juice

Maldon salt

Fresh ground white pepper

4 portions Roast Potatoes (see
  page 132)

SERVES FOUR

Heat a large frying pan until it's hot. Peel, core and quarter the apples. Season the pheasant breasts with salt and pepper.

Add 25 g (1 oz) of butter to the hot pan. When it's foaming, add the pheasant breasts and cook for three minutes each side until lightly coloured. Remove it from the heat and keep it warm.

Add the rest of the butter to the pan, then the apples and gently fry them for three to four minutes. Remove them from the heat and keep the apples warm along with the pheasant breasts.

Now add the mushrooms to the pan, increase the heat to high and stir until the mushrooms absorb the butter from the pan. Add the cider and reduce it until it's gone. Add the Stock and again reduce it this time by four-fifths.

Add the cream and bring it back to the boil. Return the pheasant breasts, the apples and any juices they have released to the pan. Add the chestnuts and warm everything through for three minutes. Add one tablespoon of the chervil and season the sauce.

To serve, lay out four warmed serving plates. Place a pheasant breast on each one and spoon over the apple, chestnuts and mushrooms. Pour the sauce over and sprinkle with the other tablespoon of chervil.

Divide the roast potatoes between the plates and serve.

PART SEVEN

BUTCHER MEAT MAIN COURSES

STEAK AND CHIPS WITH SALAD

This is what me and the wife have on our night off from the restaurant. We enjoy it with a bottle of gutsy, fruity red wine. Fiona makes the chips and salad and I do the steaks.

As ever, the best raw ingredients are all important. For the steak I tend to use the rib eye, which has the best combination of flavour and texture – but it must come from a piece of prime beef which has been well hung, preferably Aberdeen Angus.

For the chips, we use Golden Wonders when available or Cyprus. If you haven't a use for lots of salad, then supermarket packs are fine, but pick through them to find a good one.

100 g (4 oz) mixed salad leaves
25 g (1 oz) rocket and basil leaves, mixed
40 g (1½ oz) snap peas or baby asparagus
2 tablespoons sunflower oil
25 g (1 oz) unsalted butter
450 g (1 lb) Golden Wonder or Cyprus potatoes
2 × 225 g (8 oz) rib eye steaks
1 Tomato Concasse (see page 171)
1 tablespoon Vinaigrette (see page 170)
Maldon salt
Fresh ground black pepper
Cooking salt

SERVES TWO

First prepare the salad. Pick the leaves into 2.5 cm (or 1 inch) pieces and place them in a shallow bowl. Add the Concasse and the herbs.

Chop the peas or asparagus into 1 cm (½ inch) slices and add to the bowl. Refrigerate the salad until you are ready to eat.

Now make the chips. Heat a large pan with 2.5 cm (1 in) of sunflower oil until it's hot (about 190°C/375°F).

While the oil is heating up, peel the potatoes and cut them into slender chips. Add the chips to the hot oil and deep fry them, stirring several times, for six minutes.

Lift the chips out with a slotted spoon (or wire 'spider') and drain them on several thicknesses of kitchen roll. Keep them warm.

For the steaks place a large frying pan on a high heat. Season the steaks well with cooking salt and lots of fresh ground black pepper.

Add the sunflower oil to the hot frying pan. When it smokes, add the steaks, then fling in the butter and allow it to foam and cover both steaks.

After about two minutes, turn the steaks over. They should be well coloured. Cook for a further two minutes, then remove the steaks, placing them on a metal tray and leave in a warm place to rest.

Bung the chips back into the hot oil and cook until crisp and golden (it should take about two minutes) then remove to drain again.

Season the salad with crushed Maldon salt and fresh ground black pepper, add the Vinaigrette and toss it to coat.

To serve, lay out two warmed plates and place a steak on each. Pour over the meat juices, then season the chips with crushed Maldon salt and divide them between the plates.

Serve with the bowl of salad and don't forget the wine.

Relax . . .

ROAST FILLET OF BEEF WITH SHALLOTS, MUSHROOMS AND RED WINE GRAVY

Without a doubt, pure-bred Aberdeen Angus beef, properly treated and hung for at least 21 days, is the best beef you can buy. Running a close second are Galloway, Shorthorn and Highland cow. However, even the meat from a continental cross animal, when properly hung, will be fine for this dish. But *do* make the effort to get Aberdeen Angus! Ask your butcher to cut the fillets from the *centre* of the fillet. Get him to trim off the gristle and 'chain' and give you the meaty trimmings.

To make the gravy, heat a large frying pan, add one tablespoon of sunflower oil and fry the beef trimmings until browned. Add the shallot trimmings, thyme, bay leaf and crushed peppercorns and cook on a medium heat until nicely coloured. Pour in the wine and slosh it about a bit (this 'deglazes' the pan) before reducing it until all the liquid has gone.

Add the Chicken and Beef Stocks and gently simmer them until thickened. It will take approxi-

1 tablespoon sunflower oil for frying
4 x 150 g (5 oz) slices of beef fillet (keep trimmings – see introduction to recipe)
20 whole peeled shallots (keep trimmings)
1 sprig thyme
1 bay leaf

5 black peppercorns, bruised

300 ml (10 fl oz) red wine

200 ml (7 fl oz) Chicken Stock (see
page 162)

200 ml (7 fl oz) Beef Stock (see
page 163)

75 g (3 oz) cold unsalted gutter

1 tablespoon icing sugar

20 nice pieces mushroom
(chanterelle or morel, but whole
brown button will do)

1 tablespoon beef or duck fat

Maldon salt

Fresh ground black pepper

Lemon juice

SERVES FOUR

mately 30 minutes. Pass everything through a fine sieve and allow the gravy to stand. (This could be made a day in advance and left to stand overnight in the fridge). Skim the fat off the top.

Now poach the shallots in boiling seasoned water until tender (approximately ten minutes) and drain them. Fry them in 25 g (1 oz) butter with the odd dusting of icing sugar (to help the caramelisation) and continue cooking over a low to medium heat until the shallots are a good golden brown.

Keep them warm, or allow them to cool and re-heat them in a hot oven when needed. Season and add a squeeze of lemon juice just before serving.

To cook the mushrooms, heat a large frying pan until it's hot and add 25 g (1 oz) of butter. Fry the mushrooms for four to five minutes until browned. Season them with salt, pepper and lemon juice.

These may also be cooled and re-heated.

Now for the fillet. For four steaks, use two pans.

Season the steaks well with cooking salt and freshly ground black pepper. Heat the pans until very hot and add one tablespoon of Beef or Duck Fat (see page 165) or a sunflower oil and butter combination – the fat or oil should smoke. Quickly add the steaks and get some good colour on them. Two minutes on each side for good and rare. For medium or more well done, place them in a hot oven after sealing. Approximate cooking times are: Medium Rare, two to three minutes; Medium, three to four minutes; Medium Well, five to seven minutes; Well Done, ten minutes. Allow the meat to relax in a warm place for a minimum of ten minutes or a maximum of 30 minutes (when it will need 90 seconds or so in the oven to re-heat).

To serve, place the meat at one side of the plate and the Fondant Potato at the other. Arrange the shallots and mushrooms around them.

Add the remaining butter to the sauce, shake it together in the pan and season. Pour the sauce over and around the meat and mushrooms.

ROAST LEG OF LAMB WITH GARLIC AND ROSEMARY, BAKED IN FOIL AND SERVED WITH DAUPHINOISE POTATOES

During the filming of the television series, top gamekeeper Ronnie Rose showed me how he cooks a leg of Roe deer wrapped in tinfoil – and it was absolutely delicious! It was cooked for two hours and so was well done – not normally how I like my roast meat, but on this occasion I was converted.

Here, I've used a leg of lamb instead and added a few more flavours – but the idea belongs to Ronnie.

Pre-heat the oven to 190°C/375°F/Gas Mark 5.

Line a roasting pan with enough tinfoil to fold over and cover the lamb. Place the leg of lamb into this. Melt the butter in a small saucepan, then bring it to the boil. Scatter the garlic cloves and rosemary over the lamb and place the onion quarters around it. Pour on the red wine and sprinkle over the salt and pepper. Lastly, pour the boiling butter over the lamb, seal the whole thing inside the foil and bang the tray into the oven for three hours. This gives you plenty of time to make the Dauphinoise Potatoes.

When the time is up, remove the pan from the oven and leave to relax for 30 minutes in a warm place.

To serve, warm through the Dauphinoise and when ready to serve, open the tinfoil parcel (oh wow – get a smell of *that*) and lift out the lamb.

Lay out eight warmed serving plates and divide out the onion quarters and garlic bits (which will be dark and squidgy) between them.

Strain all the juices off into a pan and check the seasoning. Carve the lamb and divide out equally.

Place the Dauphinoise on the plates, then spoon over the sauce. Finally, serve and raise your glasses to toast Ronnie Rose!

3 kg (7 lb) leg of lamb, trimmed
100 g (4 oz) unsalted butter
12 cloves garlic, peeled
3 sprigs rosemary
300 ml (10 fl oz) red wine
12 turns ground white pepper
25 g (1 oz) Maldon salt, crushed
2 onions, quartered
8 porions of Dauphinoise Potatoes (see page 126)

SERVES EIGHT

Roast Fillet of Beef with Shallots,
Mushrooms and Red Wine Gravy
(page 111).

BROCHETTE OF LAMB WITH PINEAPPLE, DATES, BACON, SPICY TOMATO AND RED WINE SAUCE

I cooked this dish in my fledgling days as a chef and it's based on a recipe found in a cookbook whose name I've forgotten! What I do remember, though, is being surprised at how good it was. Brochette is just a posh term for kebab and you'll need four good, long skewers. The meat has to be marinated overnight and the sauce can also be made ahead of time and refrigerated. You can grill the kebabs, but they're also wonderful made on a barbie. If you've got a decent butcher, get him to seam bone you a couple of muscles from the leg – that way there's no gristle or waste.

I like to serve this with saffron basmati rice.

750 g–1 kg (1½–2 lb) lamb gigot (depending on the leanness of your meat), trimmed of any fat and sinew and cut into 25-g (1-oz) cubes
4 rashers streaky bacon
12 stoned dates
½ pineapple, peeled and cut into 1-cm (or ½-in) cubes
2 tablespoons olive oil

FOR THE SAFFRON RICE:
250 g (8 oz) basmati rice
1 pinch saffron strands
1½ teaspoons Maldon salt

FOR THE MARINADE:
1 teaspoon mixed spice
1 cm (½ in) chunk of bruised ginger
2 teaspoons Chilli Oil (see page 169)
1 clove garlic, mashed

Prepare the Marinade one day in advance. Mix all the ingredients together in a mixing bowl. Add the cubes of lamb (there should be approximately 24), the dates and the pineapple cubes. Mix everything well, cover with clingfilm and refrigerate for at least 12 hours or up to 24 hours.

To make the rice, pre-heat the oven to 150°C/300°F/Gas Mark 2.

In a large saucepan, bring two pints of water to the boil, adding 1½ teaspoons of salt and the saffron strands. Add the rice and stir it until it comes back to the boil. Reduce the heat and simmer for 12 minutes.

Drain the rice in a sieve and place it in a roasting tray. Leave it in the pre-heated oven for ten minutes, until it's nice and fluffy.

Alternatively, put aside to cool and re-heat it in a low oven (the same temperature as above) for 20 minutes before serving.

To make the Sauce, heat a medium-sized saucepan to a medium heat. Add half the butter and when it sizzles, add the onion, garlic and mixed spice. Gently fry everything for five minutes.

Add the tomatoes and Chilli Oil and cook it for a further five minutes. Add the red wine and reduce it until the pan is nearly dry. Add the beefstock and reduce it by about half until the sauce has thickened.

If using straight away, whisk in the remaining butter and chives and season with salt and pepper. If serving later, leave to cool and add the butter, chives and seasoning once the sauce has been reheated.

To serve, cut the bacon rashers into three pieces each and wrap the pieces around the dates. Thread up the skewers in this order — lamb, date, lamb, pineapple and so on until it's all used. Place the four skewers into a shallow roasting tray and pour any remaining marinade over the top. Place them under the grill and turn every two minutes until nicely browned (takes eight to ten minutes).

Warm through the sauce and rice and lay out four warmed serving plates. Place a bed of rice on each plate, then lay a kebab on top of each. Spoon over the warmed sauce and away you go.

2 teaspoons Maldon salt, crushed
1 teaspoon coriander seeds, crushed
1 teaspoon ground cumin
8 turns fresh ground white pepper
Zest and juice of 1 lime
1 tablespoon clear honey
1 teaspoon Worcestershire sauce

FOR THE SAUCE:
50 g (2 oz) unsalted butter
1 small onion, finely chopped
1 clove garlic, crushed
1 teaspoon mixed spice
4 plum tomatoes, peeled, seeded
   and quartered
1 teaspoon Chilli Oil (see page 169)
300 ml (10 fl oz) Beef Stock (see
   page 163)
300 ml (10 fl oz) red wine
1 tablespoon chives, chopped

SERVES FOUR

ROAST SADDLE OF LAMB WITH SPINACH AND A TOMATO AND BASIL SAUCE

Scottish lamb is wonderful. Try to get the native blackface breeds or Shetland. It's at its best from spring to summer from about the end of May until mid-September, after which it develops a more mutton like flavour. The cut I'm using here is the loin, which is a long strip of meat from alongside its backbone and in fact is the meat from the 'eye' of a lamb chop (i.e. with no bone or gristle).

Ask the butcher for one loin from a saddle of lamb. Ask him to

Roast Saddle of Lamb with Spinach
and a Tomato and Basil Sauce
(page 117) and Dauphinoise
Potatoes (page 126).

trim off all the fat and sinew, leaving you with a nice piece of lean fillet. Get the meaty trimmings and some rib bones for the sauce.

My favourite potato accompaniment to this dish is Dauphinoise (see page 126).

500 g (1¼ lb) loin of lamb (see introduction to recipe)
50 g (2 oz) unsalted butter
50–75 g (2–3 oz) meat trimmings
2 shallots, sliced
2 cloves garlic, crushed
I bay leaf
I sprig thyme
Tomato pulp (from Concasse, see below)
25 ml (I fl oz) cognac
150 ml (5 fl oz) red wine
5–6 rib bones, roasted brown
200 ml (7 fl oz) Chicken Stock (see page 162)
200 ml (7 fl oz) Beef Stock (see page 163)
200 ml (7 fl oz) water
8 large basil leaves
2 ripe plum Tomatoes Concasse (see page 171), retain pulp for sauce
100 g (4 oz) spinach leaves
2 tablespoons each sunflower oil and softened unsalted butter
Maldon salt
Fresh ground white pepper

4 portions Dauphinoise Potatoes (see page 126)

SERVES FOUR

Pre-heat the oven to 230°C/350°F/Gas Mark 8.

Make the sauce first. Heat a large frying pan until hot. Add half of the butter and when foaming brown, add the lamb trimmings, shallots, garlic, bay leaf, thyme, pepper and cook until all are well browned. Add the tomato pulp and cook it until dry. Pour in the cognac and slosh it around to deglaze the pan and then add the wine. Reduce it until all of the liquid has gone. Add the bones and stir to coat then add the stocks and the water. Bring to the boil and simmer very slowly until thickened. (This will take approximately 45 minutes). Pass the sauce through a fine sieve and keep warm.

Now roast the lamb. Season the loin with salt and fresh ground white pepper. Heat a frying pan until it's hot. Add a little of the sunflower oil and softened butter to the pan and then add the loin. Fry until well-coloured all over and place in the pre-heated hot oven for three to four minutes, depending on how pink you like your lamb, until just starting to become firm to the touch.

Allow the meat to relax in a warm place for a minimum of ten minutes before serving.

To serve, heat a large saucepan and add 25 g (1 oz) butter. Add the spinach and cook quickly. Season it and divide it between each plate. Cut three to five rounds of meat per person and place them on top of the spinach.

Add the remaining 25 g (1 oz) of the butter into the sauce and shake it until well incorporated. Chop the basil and add it along with the Concasse to the sauce.

Check the seasoning before pouring the sauce over and around the lamb and serve with Dauphinoise Potatoes.

PART EIGHT

VEGETARIAN MAIN COURSES

LASAGNE OF ROASTED RED PEPPERS, HOME DRIED TOMATOES, OLIVES, CAPERS AND A BASIL BUTTER SAUCE

One of my repertoire of vegetarian main courses. You could vary the ingredients, substituting roast courgette or aubergine for the peppers. Or try rocket, flat parsley or chives in the sauce. As usual, fresh pasta is better than dried.

8 sheets lasagne, cooked (12 × 12 cm/4 × 4 in approximately)

3 large Roasted Red Peppers (see page 174)

8 pieces Home Dried Tomato (see page 166)

16 black olives, stoned and halved

20 salted capers, rinsed and drained

25 ml (1 fl oz) olive oil

1 teaspoon Chilli Oil (see page 169), optional

175 ml (6 fl oz) Nage Butter Sauce (see page 164)

25 g (1 oz) basil leaves

25 g (1 oz) Parmesan shavings

Maldon salt

Fresh ground white pepper

Lemon juice

SERVES FOUR

Pre-heat the oven to 110°C/225°F/Gas Mark ½.

Dice the peppers into 0.5-cm (¼-in) squares. Place the peppers, tomato pieces, olives, capers, olive oil and the chilli oil into a medium saucepan. Season with salt, pepper and lemon juice.

Gently warm everything through on top of a medium-low heat for about ten minutes. Cover and keep warm (for up to one hour) in a very cool oven.

To serve, have ready a pan of salted, simmering water. In a separate pan, warm through the Nage Butter Sauce.

Roughly chop the basil and add two-thirds of it to the Nage Butter Sauce, which miraculously now becomes Basil Butter Sauce. Taste it and season if necessary.

Drop the pasta into the simmering water and heat it through for 60 seconds. Fish it out with a slotted spoon and leave it to drain on a clean teatowel.

Lay out four warmed shallow serving bowls. Place one sheet of pasta flat into the bottom of each bowl, corrugate it by pushing opposite ends together, then place an eighth of the pepper mix atop each pasta square. Now cover this with another pasta sheet, and divide out the remaining pepper mixture. Spoon the Basil Butter Sauce over this and then scatter the Parmesan shavings over the top.

Lastly, sprinkle over the remaining chopped basil and serve it to your guests, listening out for murmurs of the '. . . who needs meat?' variety.

GÂTEAU OF ROAST VEGETABLES WITH SAUCE VIERGE, PESTO AND TOMATO VINAIGRETTE

This is another favoured veggie main course. It looks quite spectacular with its two sauces. All the vegetables can be roasted in advance and reheated in the oven, leaving only the final assembly come servin' time.

Pre-heat the oven to 230°C/450°F/Gas Mark 8.

Prepare the vegetables first and have the peppers ready and cut into quarters. Wipe, top and tail the courgettes and cut each one, lengthwise, into four strips.

Wipe, top and tail the aubergine and cut it into eight discs. Lightly salt it and leave it to drain for 15 minutes. Wash it and then drain it for at least 45 minutes more, then pat dry.

Trim and quarter the fennel, taking care not to cut off too much root (if you do, it'll fall to bits).

You can roast the vegetables up to five hours before serving. To do so, heat a black iron frying pan until it's hot, add two tablespoons of olive oil, quickly followed by the fennel. Lightly fry it until it's browned all over. Season it with salt, pepper and lemon juice and then pour in 600 ml (20 fl oz) of water. Bring it to the boil and reduce the water by three quarters. Bung the pan into the hot oven for ten minutes. The fennel should be tender and most of the water absorbed.

Meanwhile fry the courgette and pepper as per the recipe for guinea fowl on page 92. Then cool all the vegetables in the fridge.

Now make the Vinaigrette. Quarter the tomatoes and liquidise them with 25 ml (1 fl oz) of olive oil. Force them through a fine sieve into a mixing bowl and season them with salt and pepper.

To make up each Gâteau, place two strips of courgette on a baking sheet. Place two rounds of

2 × Roasted Red Peppers (see page 174)

4 medium courgettes

1 large aubergine

1 medium bulb fennel

Olive oil

600 ml (20 fl oz) water

2 ripe plum tomatoes

120 ml (4 fl oz) Mediterranean Sauce Vierge

2 tablespoons Pesto (see page 167)

25 g (1 oz) rocket leaves

Sunflower oil

Maldon salt

Fresh ground white pepper

Lemon juice

SERVES FOUR

aubergine on top, then two pepper quarters. Add two more strips of courgette and top with the fennel quarter. Create three more in the same way.

To serve, warm the gâteau through in a moderate oven (160°C/325°F/Gas Mark 3) for 20 minutes.

In two small pans, warm through the Sauce Vierge and the Vinaigrette, but don't let either of them boil. Remove them from heat and keep them warm.

Place the rocket leaves in a bowl, drizzle over one teaspoon of olive oil and a few drops of lemon juice. Season with salt and pepper and toss it to coat.

Lay out four warmed plates and place a gâteau in the middle of each. Pour around a couple of spoonfuls of Vinaigrette.

Add the Pesto to the Sauce Vierge and stir. Then, to create a wonderful marbled effect with the sauces, spoon the Pesto around the plate first. The oily Pesto won't mix with the watery tomato and this will produce the desired effect.

Lastly, top with the rocket leaves and serve.

PART NINE

POTATO DISHES

DAUPHINOISE POTATOES

This recipe is based on what has been described as the Definitive Dauphinoise from one of my culinary heroes, Hilary Brown who, with her husband David, owns and runs La Potinière – which is, for me, an inspirational restaurant and a role model for Braeval.

The lovely, garlicky, creamy layers of this dish certainly demonstrate the versatility of the humble spud. But for me, one of the great advantages of dauphinoise is that it can be made in advance and reheated in individual portions on a tray. It keeps well in a cool oven. If, when reheating, you use a scone cutter to make individual rounds, your stupefied guests will wonder how on earth you managed to make these little layered potato towers!

1.25 kg (2½ lb) potatoes, preferably
  Maris Piper or similar
1 clove garlic, crushed
300 ml (10 fl oz) full cream milk
300 ml (10 fl oz) double cream
1 teaspoon Maldon salt, heaped
8 turns fresh ground white pepper
25 g (1 oz) Parmesan cheese

SERVES EIGHT

Pre-heat the oven to 150°C/300°F/Gas Mark 2.

Using the flat side of a heavy knife, crush the garlic, then mash it with half a teaspoon of salt and place in a large pan with the milk, cream and pepper and the rest of the salt. Peel and thinly slice the potatoes on a mandolin grater (or in a food processor). Place the potatoes in the pan and stir to ensure that they are fully coated with the milk and cream mixture. Bring to the boil and simmer until the potatoes are tender, stirring very gently once or twice during the cooking period, and the potato starch has thickened the milk. (This takes about 15 minutes).

Turn the potatoes out into a buttered ovenproof dish, leaving behind any burnt slices on the bottom of the pan.

Grate the Parmesan over the potatoes and bake in the cool oven for approximately one hour, until nicely browned on top. Either serve immediately or allow to cool overnight.

To reheat, cut the potatoes into squares or use a scone cutter – 6 cm (2½ in) diameter – to make rounds. Lift them out of the cutter, place on a tray and pop them into a cool oven (140°C/275°F/Gas Mark 1) for 45 minutes.

MASHED POTATOES

Mashed potatoes are a great comfort food. The secret of success in this dish lies in the quality and type of potatoes used (preferably Maris Piper or a similar waxy potato). Older spuds work better than new – and make sure that they are thoroughly cooked, but not soggy!

If you want a seriously decadent mash, double the amount of butter in the recipe. And don't add milk – unless you want it ending up runny!

Mash picks up the flavour of herbs well, especially chives and basil. A little grated Parmesan is also nice and, if you win the lottery, try some freshly grated truffle – heaven!

Pre-heat the oven to 150°C/300°F/Gas Mark 2.

Place the potatoes into a pan of salted cold water and bring to boil. As *soon* as the water comes to the boil, reduce to a simmer (it's important not to cook the potatoes too quickly), and cook for approximately 20 minutes.

Check the tenderness – the point of a sharp knife should feel little resistance when pushed into the potato.

Drain in a colander, place the potatoes on a tray and leave in the pre-heated oven for about five minutes to dry out. (Don't allow them to form a skin).

Remove the potatoes and mash them with a potato masher or pass them through a mouli or ricer into a mixing bowl.

Using a wooden spoon, beat in the butter vigorously, making the mash light and fluffy. Season and place in an ovenproof dish, covering with the butter wrapper.

The mash will keep warm in a very cool oven (120°C/250°F/Gas Mark ½) for up to three hours. Alternatively, they may be allowed to cool and be reheated gently using a little more butter. If you are using any herbs, add these approximately 10–15

450 g (1 lb) Maris Piper potatoes, peeled and quartered

40 g (1½ oz) unsalted butter (keep the wrapper handy!)

½ teaspoon Maldon salt

6 turns freshly ground white pepper

SERVES FOUR

minutes before serving. This gives enough time for the potato to take on the flavour, but for the herbs to keep their colour.

ROSTI POTATOES

Slightly tricky to make, but worth it. Crispy on the outside, soft and buttery on the inside, you should always make them in advance and reheat them, since trying to do them to order can be a tense experience. Use Golden Wonder, Cyprus or another starchy potato.

450 g (1 lb) Golden Wonder or
 Cyprus potatoes, peeled
75 ml (3 fl oz) Clarified Butter (see
 page 175)
½ teaspoon Maldon salt
6 turns fresh ground white pepper

SERVES FOUR

Grate the potatoes (using a box grater) onto a clean tea towel. Wring out the excess moisture by twisting the towel into a tight ball shape. Place the dried potato into a bowl and add 25 ml (1 fl oz) of the clarified butter and season. You will need to do this quickly or the potato will start to discolour.

Heat the remaining Clarified Butter in a medium-sized 20-cm (8-in) frying pan. Add the potato mix, pushing down with a spatula to ensure that it evenly covers the pan.

Cook at a medium temperature for about eight to ten minutes until you see traces of colour at the edges, then turn over and cook until the Rosti is golden coloured on both sides (about three to four minutes). Drain on a wire rack. When cooled, cut into quarters.

The Rosti may be made up to six hours in advance and left at room temperature until ready to use. They can be re-heated in a moderate oven (180°C/350°F/Gas Mark 4) for five minutes.

BOULANGÈRE POTATOES

This is best made a day ahead and it is important to make sure that the potatoes are thoroughly cooked and all the stock is absorbed.

Pre-heat the oven to 175°C/300°F/Gas Mark 4.

Use 25 g (1 oz) of the butter to grease a shallow roasting tin. Scatter one third of the onions in the bottom, followed by one third of the potatoes. Season them and repeat this layering process three times making sure no onions are on the top layer.

Dot the remaining butter over the top and pour over the chicken stock.

Bake in the oven for one hour until the potatoes are lightly browned on top. If, after 40 minutes, the top is browning but the potatoes aren't cooked, you can cover the dish with foil and leave it in the oven until they are done.

450 g (1 lb) potatoes, peeled and thinly sliced
225 g (8 oz) onions, thinly sliced
50 g (2 oz) unsalted butter
300 ml (10 fl oz) Chicken Stock (see page 162)
Maldon salt
Fresh ground white pepper

SERVES SIX

FONDANT POTATO

This is a very rich and tasty potato dish, similar to the Galette (see opposite), but more moist. It works well with Maris Piper, but they'll have to be large baking spuds.

2 large baking potatoes
73 g (3 oz) unsalted butter
Maldon salt
Fresh ground white pepper

YOU WILL ALSO NEED:
1 ovenproof frying pan,
  approximately 15 cm (6 in)
  diameter, (see page 9)
1 scone cutter (6 cm/2¼ in)

SERVES FOUR

Pre-heat the oven to 190°C/375°F/Gas Mark 5.

Wash the spuds and cut them in half across their narrowest width. Slice off the tops, so you're left with cylindrical sections of spud 2.5 cm (1 in) thick.

Place these on your chopping board and use the scone cutter to stamp out a cylinder of potato. You can trim the sharp edges of the cylinders with a potato peeler (this helps to prevent them sticking to the pan). Repeat this with the other bits until you have four potato discs.

Line the base of the ovenproof frying pan with the butter. I know it looks a lot! Now squish the potato discs into the butter and season with a little salt and pepper.

Pour on enough water to come three quarters of the way up the potato (don't cover the tops), whack it onto your gas ring or electric hob and bring to the boil. Reduce the heat and simmer for 15 minutes. The water and butter will be nearly all gone (having been soaked up into the spuds).

Turn the discs over *carefully* with a spatula. You'll notice that the bottoms have started to brown. This is a good thing. Also, they'll smell great.

Now stick the ovenproof frying pan into the pre-heated oven and cook for a further 20 to 25 minutes. (This means checking it — when they're dark brown and crispy looking, they're ready to come out.)

Allow the potatoes to stand for ten minutes before serving. You can also, however, let them cool in the pan and set aside (for up to 12 hours), then reheat them in the oven (180°C/350°F/Gas Mark 4) for ten minutes.

POTATO GALETTE

This is a potato dish for the adventurous. More complicated than most, but get it right and it's potato sex! A crisp, brown shell containing a moist, buttery interior — just like a great, big chip! Needless to say, not one for dieters.

Pre-heat the oven to 200°C/400°F/Gas Mark 6.

Peel and halve the potatoes. Using a scone cutter, press into each half to form a cylinder. Using a sharp knife or a mandolin grater, slice each cylinder into 9 × 3-mm (⅛-in) thick sections.

Blanch the slices in boiling, salted water for three to four minutes. Remove them with a slotted spoon and pat dry on a tea towel (don't rinse off the starch — that way they'll stick together more easily).

Season each disc lightly — you could also place a tiny sprig of thyme on each one if you like the flavour.

Divide the melted clarified butter among the ramekins, then press the potato discs in three at a time. They should just reach the tops of the ramekins.

Half fill a roasting tray with sunflower oil and place the ramekins into the tray (this is a sort of oil Bain Mairie and protects the potato from burning).

NB: Be very careful when taking the tray out of the oven as the oil will be very hot and if you spill it on yourself you could get a nasty burn.

Bake for about 20 minutes until browned on top and soft all the way through (insert the tip of a sharp knife for this — it should meet little resistance).

At this stage, the galettes can be kept warm for up to 40 minutes before turning them out for serving. They can also keep for up to six hours if left to cool, and then reheated in a medium oven (180°C/350°F/Gas Mark 4) for 20 minutes before serving.

2 large baking potatoes
85 ml (3 fl oz) melted Clarified
  Butter (see page 175)
Maldon salt
Fresh ground white pepper
Boiling, salted water
4 tiny sprigs thyme (optional)
Olive oil

YOU WILL ALSO NEED:

4 × 100 ml/3½ oz No. 2 ramekins
1 scone cutter, the same size as the
  ramekins

SERVES FOUR

Keep the galettes in the ramekins until the last minute. When turning them out, do it over a tray to catch any excess Clarified Butter (which you don't want all over your serving plates, or burning your fingers!)

ROAST POTATOES

4 × large Golden Wonder potatoes
  (or similar)
1.2 litres (2 pints) sunflower oil
Maldon salt
White pepper

SERVES FOUR

Pre-heat the oven to 200°C/400°F/Gas Mark 6.

Wrap the potatoes individually in foil and place them on a baking tray. Bake them in the oven for approximately 1½ hours until they are cooked through. Allow them to cool and then peel and cut each potato into four pieces.

Heat the oil to 180°C/350°F. Season the potatoes with salt and pepper and deep-fry them for about eight minutes or until they are golden brown, taking care not to overcook them. Drain them on kitchen paper for one minute and serve immediately.

PART TEN

PUDDINGS

ORANGE GRANITA WITH STRAWBERRIES

Granite (or water ices, as they are also known) are a kind of crunchy sorbet. They are very easy to make and don't require any fancy equipment. This recipe also has the benefit of no added sugar, making it a good pudding for dieters. The granita needs a little patience during making, but once made keeps for up to three weeks in the freezer.

4 juicy oranges
450 g (1 lb) ripe strawberries

SERVES FOUR

Squeeze the juice from the oranges and pour it into a shallow metal bowl. Place this in the freezer and remove at 30-minute intervals, giving it a mix with a wooden spoon. Do this over a four-hour period. Each stirring will break the ice crystals down into ever smaller particles until you end up with a crunchy sorbet texture.

If you forget one of these stages, the best way to recover the texture is to remove the mix from the freezer, let it partially thaw, and then bung it into the food processor for a quick whizz. Then carry on as per my instructions.

To serve, slice the strawberries in half lengthwise leaving the green top in place. Lay them around the edges of four cold serving plates, cut side facing out. Pile the granite in the centre, dividing equally between the plates. Serve.

Simple.

ARMAGNAC PARFAIT WITH PRUNES AND EARL GREY SYRUP

This simple, elegant dish is the ultimate standby dessert – but it has to be prepared at least 12 hours in advance and the prunes have to be soaked for at least 24 hours before use. The cleverness of this dish is that not only does the Armagnac flavour the parfait, it also acts as an anti-freeze, allowing you to serve it straight from the freezer.

This is basically an ice cream, but the prune syrup adds a contrast of temperature – which I love in desserts. The parfait keeps for up to 14 days in the freezer.

For the Earl Grey Syrup, bring the Stock Syrup to the boil. Add the tea leaves and allow to infuse for six minutes.

Pass the syrup through a sieve (basically using it as a big tea strainer) and add the prunes to the still-hot liquid. Season with the lemon juice and 25 ml (1 fl oz) of the Armagnac.

Place this in a tub, allow it to cool, and then store in the fridge. These could be used straight away, but does improve the longer you leave them.

For the Armagnac Parfait, whisk the egg yolks in an electric mixer until very pale and well risen in volume. Whip the cream with the rest of the Armagnac until it just starts to thicken.

Boil the caster sugar and three tablespoons of water until it reaches softball stage (*i.e.* dip in a cold spoon, coating it, dip this into cold water to set and pinch a little between finger and thumb. When it can be rolled into a soft ball, it's ready).

With the mixer running on full speed, slowly pour the softball sugar onto the yolks. Reduce the speed by half and whisk for a further five minutes.

Fold the yolk and syrup mix and the whipped cream together and pour it into the individual dariole moulds. Freeze immediately.

To serve, heat four prunes per person in enough Earl Grey Syrup to cover.

600 ml (20 fl oz) Stock Syrup (see page 178)
1 tablespoon Earl Grey tealeaves
32 Agen prunes, soaked in cold water for 24 hours and stoned
5 egg yolks
300 ml (10 fl oz) double cream
75 ml (3 fl oz) good Armagnac
75 g (3 oz) caster sugar, dissolved in 3 tablespoons water
1 tablespoon lemon juice
12 × 125 ml (5 fl oz) dariole moulds

MAKES TWELVE

Remove the Parfaits from freezer, run the tip of a knife around the top of each one, invert the moulds and give them a good old tap on a hard surface to help release them.

Turn the Parfaits out onto the centre of each plate. Arrange four prunes around each one and drizzle a little Earl Grey Syrup over.

Serve.

NB: You could just pour the parfait mix into a tub, freeze it and use an icecream scoop to serve it.

KIRSCH PARFAIT WITH COCONUT BISCUIT AND PINEAPPLE SAUCE

This works on the same principle as the Armagnac Parfait (see page 135), flavoured this time with kirsch, a liqueur made from cherry stones. Parfait is an ice cream which doesn't need churning, making it ideal for those folks who don't have an ice cream machine.

The biscuits can be made 24 hours in advance and kept in an airtight container, and the pineapple sauce keeps for three days in the fridge.

FOR THE PARFAIT:
8 egg yolks, size 3
75 ml (3 fl oz) kirsch
100 g (4 oz) sugar, dissolved in 4 tablespoons water
450 ml (¾ pint) double cream
8 x 125 ml (5 fl oz) dariole moulds

FOR THE COCONUT BISCUITS (MAKES 16):
150 g (5 oz) caster sugar
125 g (4½ oz) desiccated coconut
2 egg whites, size 2
75 g (3 oz) unsalted butter, melted

Make the Parfaits following the same method as for Armagnac Parfaits (on page 135).

In summary: Whisk the egg yolks until pale. Boil the sugar syrup to a soft ball. Whisk the cream and kirsch to a ribbon. Pour the sugar syrup onto the yolks. Fold the yolks and cream together. Pour into the moulds. Freeze for 12 hours.

To make the Coconut Biscuits, place the sugar, coconut and egg whites together in a mixing bowl and give them a good, frenzied beat with a wooden spoon. Pour in the melted butter and beat everything again. Chill the mix for a minimum of three hours. (The mix keeps for up to ten days in the fridge if that makes life easier.)

To make the Coconut Biscuits, pre-heat the oven to 190°C/375°F/Gas Mark 5.

Line a baking sheet with non-stick parchment paper then make 16 ping pong size balls with the coconut mix and place these on the baking sheet. Press each one down until they are approximately 5 mm (¼ in) thick.

Cook them in the oven for about 10–12 minutes until pale golden brown, then lift them off with a spatula and allow to cool for 20 minutes on a rack.

To make the Pineapple Sauce, use a sharp knife, cut away the outer skin of the pineapple. Cut the flesh in half and cut out the hard centre.

Roughly chop the flesh and place it in a liquidiser goblet with the Stock Syrup. Whizz for one minute, pour it into a plastic jug or bowl and leave until required.

To serve, lay out eight cold plates. On each one, place two coconut biscuits to one side. Turn out the Parfaits to sit half on/half off the biscuits.

Pour around the pineapple sauce and serve.

FOR THE PINEAPPLE SAUCE:

½ ripe pineapple

25 ml (1 fl oz) Stock Syrup (see page 178)

SERVES EIGHT

LEFT: Strawberry Pavlova with
Raspberry Sauce (page 141).
RIGHT: Armagnac Parfait with
Prunes and Earl Grey Syrup
(page 135).

GRAND MARNIER PARFAIT WITH A SALAD OF PINK GRAPEFRUIT AND ORANGES WITH A CITRUS SYRUP

The ubiquitous parfait is this time flavoured with Grand Marnier, a citrus salad and a zingy sauce.

FOR THE PARFAIT:

5 egg yolks, size 3
75 ml (3 fl oz) Grand Marnier
75 g (3 oz) sugar, dissolved in
   50 ml (2 fl oz) water
300 ml (10 fl oz) double cream
8 individual dariole moulds

FOR THE SALAD:

3 ripe, pink grapefruit
3 juicy oranges

FOR THE CITRUS SYRUP:

20 g (¾ oz) arrow root
25 g (1 oz) caster sugar
300 ml (10 fl oz) reserved citrus
   juice

SERVES EIGHT

Make the Sauce first by cutting all the skin and pith from the oranges and grapefruit with a small sharp knife. Now cut out the individual fruit segments from the orange and grapefruit – *i.e.* from between the pith membranes – so that, once the segments are cut out, you are left with a kind of fruit pith 'skeleton'. Place the cut out fruit segments in a tub and refrigerate.

Place a sieve over a mixing bowl and squeeze the remaining juice from the pith (which will still have some pulp left on) into the sieve to collect in the bowl.

Measure out the juice (you should have 300 ml/½ pint). Add 20 g (¾ oz) of arrowroot and the sugar. Whisk together and pour it into a small saucepan.

Place the saucepan on a medium heat and bring it to the boil, whisking all the time. The juice should thicken just before the sauce comes to the boil. Skim off any scum and place the sauce in the fridge until cooled.

Make the Parfait in the same way as described on page 135 but replacing the Kirsch with Grand Marnier.

To serve, place a pile of the mixed fruit segments to one side of a cold plate. Unmould the Parfait and place it on the other side of the plate. Spoon over two to three tablespoons of sauce per portion. Serve.

STRAWBERRY PAVLOVA WITH RASPBERRY SAUCE

This is easy peasy. The Pavlova bases can be made up to seven days ahead. I make a big pavlova, then cut it into squares – which is not only easy to do but looks different from the common or garden variety. Instead of strawberries and raspberries you can try it with any berries which are in season – or even with pineapple, Kiwi fruit or nectarines.

Ideally, the meringue base should have a texture like marshmallow.

Pre-heat the oven to 160°C/310°F/Gas Mark 2½.

To make the meringue, whisk the egg whites in a mixer until they start to thicken. At this point, add the sugar a little at a time until fully incorporated. *But be careful* – add the sugar too soon and the meringue won't bulk up enough, too late and it will split.

When all the sugar has been added, pour in the lemon juice and cornflour mix. Whisk again on full speed for six to eight minutes until the meringue is thick and shiny.

Line a shallow baking tin (15 cm × 10 cm × 2.5 cm/6 in × 4 in × 1 in) with a little oil and greaseproof paper. Spoon the meringue into the tin and smooth it down with a palette knife.

Bake it in the pre-heated oven for 45 minutes until slightly risen and browned on top.

To make the Raspberry Sauce, place the raspberries, icing sugar and one tablespoon of lemon juice in a blender and whizz for 45 seconds. Pass the mixture through a fine sieve into a bowl. Refrigerate it until required.

When the meringue is baked, remove it from the oven, allow it to cool for approximately two hours and then turn it out onto a tray (the same size if possible). If you want to store the base, wrap it in clingfilm and keep at room temperature for up to 4 days.

150 g (5 oz) egg whites (approx. 4–5), size 3
225 g (8 oz) caster sugar
1 tablespoon lemon juice and 1 heaped teaspoon cornflour, mixed together
350 g (8 oz) raspberries
25 g (1 oz) icing sugar
1 tablespoon lemon juice
450 ml (15 fl oz) double cream
350 g (12 oz) strawberries, halved

SERVES SIX

To serve, whisk the double cream until it reaches a soft peak but be careful not to overwork it. Now remove the greaseproof paper and, using a spatula, spread the cream over the pavlova and smooth it with a palette knife to form a clean shape with a flat top.

Using a thin, sharp knife, divide the Pavlova into six equal parts. Lift them out and decorate them with the halved strawberries. Place the Pavlova on to six serving plates and pour round the Raspberry Sauce. Serve.

STRAWBERRY FOOL

This is an incredibly easy pudding, best made in the summer when the strawberries are cheap and at their best. You can jazz it up a bit by adding four crushed Amaretti biscuits to the mix. Serve this up in four of your nicest glasses.

275 g (10 oz) ripe strawberries, hulled
25 g (1 oz) caster sugar
1 tablespoon Grand Marnier
300 ml (10 fl oz) double cream

SERVES FOUR

Place the hulled strawberries with the sugar and Grand Marnier into a medium-sized mixing bowl and crush everything together with a fork. Don't overwork this – you want a nice stodgy mass, not a purée.

In a separate bowl, lightly whip the cream and fold it in to the strawberry mix.

To serve, pour the fool into the serving glasses and refrigerate for one hour before serving.

SWEET PASTRY AND BLIND-BAKED FLAN

You need to know how to make the first one in order to make and enjoy the second. And you *will* enjoy it!

Cream the butter, sugar and salt at a medium speed in the bowl of a food mixer. When light and fluffy, add 50 g (2 oz) of flour. With the mixer on a lower speed, add the egg yolk and the remaining flour a tablespoon at a time. When the mix is fully incorporated, add the water and mix it for a further 15 seconds.

Remove the bowl from the mixer, tip out the dough onto a floured worktop and with floured hands, gently knead the dough three or four times until it comes together. Wrap it in clingfilm and allow it to rest in the fridge for at least three hours before rolling it out.

For the Blind-Baked Flan, pre-heat the oven at 200°C/400°F/Gas Mark 6.

Take the sweet paste from the fridge and place it on a floured worktop. Roll out until the pastry is about 3 mm (⅛ inch) thick. Cut it into a circular shape, slightly larger than the diameter of the flan ring.

Press the pastry down into the shape of the flan ring, folding the edges over the top of the ring, and place it on a baking sheet. Line the flan with clingfilm and fill it with baking beans. (I use dried peas or butterbeans).

Place it into the fridge and leave for 15 minutes before baking it in the oven for 11 minutes.

Take it from the oven, remove the clingfilm and the beans and then place it back in the oven. Bake it for a further nine minutes until the bottom is lightly browned.

Remove it and leave it to cool until required.

180 g (6 oz) unsalted butter
60 g (2 oz) sugar
Pinch of salt
250 g (9 oz) plain flour
1 egg yolk, size 3
1 tablespoon cold water

YOU WILL ALSO NEED:
1 × 25 cm (10 in) flan ring
1 rolling pin
Clingfilm
Baking beans

MAKES ENOUGH FOR ONE 25-CM (10-IN) BLIND-BAKED FLAN

GLAZED BAKED LEMON TART

If you get this spot on it's the perfect pudding. You should aim for a thin, crisp layer of caramel on top with a soft, tangy lemon filling and a crumbly crunchy pastry bottom.

For the best 'lemony' flavour from the following mixture, prepare it two days in advance and keep it refrigerated. This isn't essential, but does give a more distinctive result. To glaze, I use my blowtorch – but a wee spell under your grill will do just as well.

1 Blind-Baked Flan (see page 143)
3 juicy lemons (unwaxed if possible)
275 g (10 oz) caster sugar
6 eggs, size 3
300 ml (10 fl oz) double cream

SERVES EIGHT TO TEN

Grate the lemon zest into a bowl. Add the lemon juice, sugar and eggs and whisk until well incorporated. Then combine the cream with the lemon mixture and then pour it into a tall jug. Cover with clingfilm and refrigerate it until required but preferably for at least two days.

On the day you want to eat it, pre-heat the oven to 150–75°C/300–50°F/Gas Mark 2–3.

Place the Blind-Baked flan onto a baking sheet and put it into oven.

Remove the lemon mixture from the fridge and skim off any froth from the top before giving it a stir.

Pull the rack with the flan on it partially out of the oven and pour the mix into the flan until it fills to the top. I do it this way so as to have the minimum of movement when the flan is full of mixture (you don't want this stuff on your floor).

Bake the tart for 25 minutes. It has to be cooked until just set – *i.e.* with no 'wobble' in the centre.

To serve, remove the tart and allow it to cool. Trim the pastry around the top edges before removing the flan ring. Cut the tart into eighths, dust it with icing sugar and glaze it with a blow torch or under the grill.

Serve it with double cream. It's a heavenly wee taste!

CRÈME BRULÉE – MY WAY

I know that everybody and their auntie makes crème brulée. But this version ain't the usual custard set-a-bain-marie-in-the-oven-routine, which I find makes the brulées too heavy. This method involves incorporating air into the egg yolks, giving lightness to the mixture. Plus, it's quicker.

Use the best quality vanilla pods – Bourbon if you can get them.

Heat the cream, vanilla pod and seeds together in a pot to just below boiling. Place a whisking bowl over a separate pan of simmering water. Add the yolks and sugar to the bowl and whisk until they become thick. This should take five to six minutes.

Bring the cream to the boil and, just as it starts to rise up through the pan, pour two thirds into the whisking bowl with the eggs. Whisk them together thoroughly, then pour the mix back into the pot with the remaining cream. (Another pair of hands would be useful here – ask a friend.)

Place the bowl back on the heat and stir the mixture with a wooden spoon for one or two minutes until mix thickens sufficiently.

Remove the pan from the heat and continue stirring for a further couple of minutes. Divide the mix between the six ramekins, filling them to the brim. Allow the mixture to set in the fridge for at least six hours or preferably overnight.

To serve, dust the surface of the brulées with some icing sugar (a teastrainer is good for this). Then apply the heat of a blowlamp to glaze. Alternatively, if you aren't brave enough, place the brulées under a hot grill, but watch them like a hawk because they burn very easily.

When glazed, they should be a nice mahogany brown colour – but *don't* poke your fingers into the brulée top. Burny, burny sugar – ouch!

Place the brulées in the fridge for three minutes before serving.

600 ml (20 fl oz) double cream
1 vanilla pod, split lengthwise, seeds
  scooped out and kept
6 egg yolks, size 3
75 g (3 oz) caster sugar
3 tablespoons icing sugar
6 × 150 ml/¼ pint/No. 1 ramekins

SERVES SIX

LEFT: Chocolate Soufflé Pudding
with Cinnamon Ice Cream and
Hot Chocolate Sauce (page 149).
RIGHT: Chocolate Tart with
Whisky Cream (page 148).

CHOCOLATE TART WITH WHISKY CREAM

A fabulous desert – it took me ages to perfect this recipe. This requires seriously good quality dark chocolate with 60% cocoa solids or more. I use chocolate pistoles, which are up-market choc drops.

Although best served still warm, it's still pretty damn good the next day (if there's any left).

100 g (4 oz) unsalted butter
225 g (8 oz) chocolate pistoles or grated chocolate
3 whole eggs, size 3
3 egg yolks, size 3
50 g (2 oz) caster sugar
1 × 25-cm (10-inch) Blind-Baked flan (see page 143)
300 ml (10 fl oz) whipping cream
1 tablespoon caster sugar (for the cream)
2 tablespoons your favourite malt whisky

SERVES TEN PEOPLE (OR EIGHT PIGGIES)

Pre-heat the oven to 180°C/350°F/Gas Mark 4.

Put the butter and chocolate together in a stainless steel bowl and place it over a pan of simmering water. Gently melt the chocolate and butter together, stirring from time to time with a wooden spoon. The mix should be dark and glossy. Remove the bowl and keep warm.

Into another bowl, place the eggs and whisk these over the simmering water until pale and fluffy. Add the sugar and whisk for a further three minutes until thick and frothy.

Fold the egg and the chocolate mixes together and then pour the mixture into the flan. Place it into the pre-heated oven and bake it for about 20 minutes.

When it is baked, the tart should be lightly risen around the edges and firm in the centre. Allow it to cool a little before you turn it out.

Whip the cream and flavour with the caster sugar and malt whisky and refrigerate until you are ready.

To serve, cut the tart into 10 (or 8!) slices, serving each with a dollop of the whipped cream.

CHOCOLATE SOUFFLÉ/CHOCOLATE MOUSSE/CHOCOLATE SOUFFLÉ PUDDING

Three boffo desserts for the price of one! This mixture is (as you might have gathered) extremely versatile. It can be served hot as a soufflé, or left to set in the fridge, where it becomes a fabulously rich, dark chocolate mousse.

Your third alternative, should you desire, is to leave them to stand for 5 minutes once they're out of the oven, allowing them to sink back into the ramekins. They can be turned out and served with hot chocolate sauce and whipped cream to make most excellent warm chocolate pudding!

The uncooked soufflé mix can be prepared up to 45 minutes in advance and kept at room temperature before baking. They won't rise quite as well, but are just as delicious!

Pre-heat the oven to 220°C/425°F/Gas Mark 7.

Melt the chocolate in a mixing bowl placed over a saucepan of simmering water. When completely melted, beat in the egg yolks with a wooden spoon until the mixture becomes thick and stiff.

In the food mixer, whisk the egg whites until they start to thicken. At this point, add all of the sugar and continue to whisk for about three minutes until the meringue becomes thick and smooth. It should just come to soft peaks.

Whisk about one-fifth of the meringue into the chocolate and yolk mix and then carefully fold in the remaining meringue. You need to retain as much volume as possible, since it is the trapped air in the mix which makes the soufflé rise.

Divide the mixture into the ramekins and give each one a good tap to flatten the surface. There is no need to smooth the top. Bake them in the oven for 12 to 13 minutes until they've risen well. Dust each one with icing sugar and serve with a dollop of whipped cream flavoured with the cognac.

FOR THE SOUFFLÉS:
300 g (11 oz) dark chocolate
  (should be 60% cocoa solids)
4 egg yolks, size 3
250 ml (8 fl oz) egg whites
100 g (4 oz) caster sugar
12 ramekins, lined with butter and
  sugar

FOR SERVING:
150 ml (5 fl oz) whipped cream
1 tablespoon Cognac
1 teaspoon icing sugar

FOR THE CHOCOLATE SAUCE IF SERVING HOT:
100 g (4 oz) dark chocolate, grated
3 tablespoons milk

MAKES TWELVE

Any remaining, uncooked mixture may be kept in a container in the fridge to be used purely as a chocolate mousse.

If you want to serve them as hot chocolate puddings, melt together the dark chocolate with the milk on a low heat, stirring continuously with a wooden spoon until you have a glossy chocolate sauce to pour over the puddings.

Two little pots

The idea for this came from one of our regular customers at *Braeval*. She had just returned from Paris and was raving on about a pudding that she'd tasted in Joel Robuchon's Brasserie. Just two little pots – one chocolatey and the other vanilla. So simple and yet so wonderful (she said). Not to be outdone in superlatives by the French, I've used my Brulée recipe (see page 145) for the vanilla pot and nicked one of Hilary Brown's (of La Potinière fame) recipes for the choccy one. Shameless, me.

FOR THE VANILLA POTS:

Follow the ingredients and method for Crème Brulée using half the quantity (see page 145), except pour the mix into six 75-ml (3-fl oz) ramekins (No. 3 size) when you're done

FOR THE CHOCOLATE POTS:

175 g (6 oz) dark chocolate, grated
120 ml (4 fl oz) double cream
120 ml (4 fl oz) full cream milk
1 whole egg, size 3
6 x 75-ml (3-fl oz) ramekins (No. 3 size)

SERVES SIX

I'll assume you've made the Vanilla Pots so now make the chocolate ones.

Place the chocolate into a food processor. Pour the cream and milk into a medium-sized saucepan and bring it to the boil. Once boiled, add this to the food processor, wait for 30 seconds and then whizz it all together for 30 seconds.

Add the egg (having first broken it open and discarded the shell, I must add), and whizz everything for a further 45 seconds.

Pour the mix into a jug and carefully fill the six ramekins with the mixture. Place them in the fridge and allow them to set overnight.

To serve, place one Vanilla pot and one Chocolate pot onto each serving plate, side by side. And there you have it, two little pots!

(That'll teach the French.)

CARAMELISED APPLE TART

This is a really tasty marriage of apple and caramel custard. It is best served warm with a dollop of whipped cream or crème fraîche and can be reheated the next day. This is the kind of dessert that gets a lot of 'oohs' and 'aahs' at the restaurant.

Place the sugar into a large frying pan and put it onto a medium heat. Allow the sugar to melt slowly and stir as little as possible, only doing so to fold in little areas of dark caramel which will start to appear.

After six to eight minutes all of the sugar will be melted, and this is what is known as a blonde caramel. What you need is a dark caramel, so allow the sugar to cook a little further (another two to three minutes should do). The caramel is ready when it has large bubbles appearing on the surface and starts to release a dark, acrid smoke.

Remove the pan from heat and carefully tip in all the apples, being careful that the caramel doesn't splash. Since hot, melted sugar can give you a very nasty burn indeed, you could play safe by wearing rubber gloves for this stage.

Mix everything together with a wooden spoon. Once the apples are coated in the caramel, carefully pour in the cream (watch it, because it will boil and sputter) and place the pan back onto the heat, stirring for about three minutes until all of the caramel is dissolved.

Pour the contents of the pan into a sieve set over a mixing bowl and allow the sieved mix to cool for 30 minutes. During this time pre-heat the oven to 160°C/325°F/Gas Mark 3.

When you are ready to serve, arrange the apple segments in the bottom of the Blind-Baked Flan. Add the eggs to the caramel liquid and gently whisk them in.

Place the flan onto a baking sheet, strain the caramel custard onto the flan through a sieve and

275 g (10 oz) caster sugar
6 Granny Smith apples, peeled and
   quartered, with each quarter cut
   into 3
300 ml (10 fl oz) double cream
1 x 23-cm (9-in) Blind-Baked Flan
   (see page 143)
3 whole eggs, size 3

SERVES EIGHT

place it into the oven for 35 to 45 minutes until it has just risen around the edges and the centre has set.

Remove the flan and allow it to cool slightly before turning it out and dividing it into eight portions. Serve warm with whipped cream.

POACHED PEAR WITH VANILLA CREAM PASTRY AND CHAMPAGNE SYRUP

You don't *have* to use champagne – any old fizzy wine will do, but *do* buy the best quality puff pastry that you can get, preferably one made with butter. (For some masochistic reason, I still insist on making my own at the restaurant, but quality bought stuff is nearly as good).

When buying the pears, pick ones that are just under ripe. I prefer to use comice pears for their shape and flavour.

This recipe is a little complex and needs planning. You can make the pears up to four days in advance, but the pastry and cream should be made up in the morning.

FOR THE PEARS:
450 g (15 oz) granulated sugar
450 ml (15 fl oz) champagne (or
  sparkling wine)
4 comice pears
Juice of ½ lemon

To poach the pears, mix the 450 g (15 oz) sugar and the champagne or sparkling wine in a medium-sized saucepan. Bring it to the boil, stirring from time to time.

Peel the pears (using a potato peeler), leaving on the stalk. Using a melon baller, scoop out the seeds and pith from the bottom of the pears before placing them into the boiling syrup, stalks upwards. Bring it back to the boil.

Remove the pan from the heat and add the lemon juice. Allow it to cool with the pears still immersed in the syrup and set it aside until required.

These are best made 24 hours in advance.

For the Vanilla Cream, pour the milk into a small pan, split the halved vanilla pod down its length and add it to the milk. Place this on a low heat and warm it through until nearly boiling.

In a small mixing bowl, whisk together the sugar, egg yolk, plain flour and cornflour until smooth. Pour this mixture into the hot milk and whisk everything together.

Scrape this out of the bowl and into the pan and cook it over a low heat for three to five minutes, stirring continuously until the mix has thickened. Leave it aside to cool.

Whisk the double cream until it thickens to a soft peak. Then remove the vanilla pod from the cooled milk mixture and fold the cream and milk mixture together until fully incorporated. Keep it in the fridge until needed.

To make the pastry, pre-heat the oven to 200°C/ 400°F/Gas Mark 6.

Roll the pastry out to 5 mm (¼ inch) thickness. Cut it into four squares, approximately 4 cm × 4 cm (1½ × 1½ in). Place them on a baking sheet and refrigerate for 15 minutes.

Remove them from the fridge and use the back of a fork to mark some stripes on top of each pastry. Paint each one with eggwash, and then bake them in the oven for 15 minutes until risen and well browned.

Leave to cool on a rack until required.

To serve, lay out four serving plates. Split each pastry in half and scoop out any soggy pastry from inside. Stuff the cavities with the Vanilla Cream and replace the tops.

Place a pastry and a pear side by side on each plate and drizzle over a little of the champagne syrup.

FOR THE VANILLA CREAM PASTRY:

85 ml (3 fl oz) milk
½ a vanilla pod, preferably Bourbon
15 g (½ oz) granulated sugar
1 egg yolk, size 3
1 teaspoon cornflour
1 teaspoon plain flour
120 ml (4 fl oz) double cream
175 g (6 oz) quality puff pastry
Eggwash (1 yolk and 1 tablespoon milk)

SERVES FOUR

LEFT: Passion Fruit Jelly with
Fresh Fruits (page 156).
RIGHT: Poached Pear with
Vanilla Cream Pastry and
Champagne Syrup (page 152).

PASSION FRUIT JELLY WITH FRESH FRUITS

This may seem like a bit of a 'footer' (for those not familiar with Scots' idiom, it's from the French 'foutre' – look it up) to make – but wait until it passes across your tastebuds!

Lots of people are put off using gelatine because they think it's going to go all lumpy and horrid on them. This will only occur if you use common or garden powdered gelatine – so buy leaf gelatine. It's better and easier to use.

You could vary the fruits, but after years of trying various combos out, this recipe is as good as it gets for me.

Note that the 'jelly' has to be made at least one day before.

2 leaves gelatine

16 passion fruits

175 ml (6 fl oz) Stock Syrup (see page 178)

1 ripe paw paw

1 ripe mango

1 orange

1 lime

100 g (4 oz) strawberries

4 × 75 ml (3 fl oz) dariole moulds

SERVES FOUR

To make the Fruit Jelly, 24 hours in advance, half fill a bowl with cold water. Add the gelatine leaves and soak them for 15 minutes until softened and easy to use. Halve 14 of the passion fruits and use a teaspoon to gouge out the seeds and flesh into a liquidiser goblet. Give them a quick whizz (about 45 seconds) then tip the whole lot into a fine sieve and use the back of a small ladle to force all the juice out into a bowl.

Pour all of this into a measuring jug. You should have near as dammit 200 ml (7 fl oz) liquid. Make up any difference with some freshly squeezed orange juice.

Place 125 ml (4¼ fl oz) of the Stock Syrup in a small saucepan and bring it to the boil before removing it from heat.

Take the gelatine leaves from the cool water and squeeze out any excess liquid. Ease this into the hot syrup and swirl it around in the pan until it's dissolved. Pour in the passion fruit juice and mix together well.

Pour the liquid into the dariole moulds and refrigerate overnight until set.

Next prepare the fruits which you can do up to five days in advance.

Using a small, sharp knife, peel the paw paw, mango and orange. Cut the paw paw in half and scoop out the seeds. Keep two teaspoons for the garnish.

Cut the mango away from the stone and dice the flesh into 1 cm (½ in) chunks. Cut the orange segments out and place them in a bowl with the mango and paw paw. Squeeze over the remaining juice from the orange and add the juice from the lime.

Sprinkle the remaining 50 ml (2 fl oz) of Stock Syrup over it and mix gently. Pour it into a tub and refrigerate it until required.

To serve, have a bowl of hot water ready and four cold serving plates.

Dip the dariole moulds into the hot water for five seconds, then invert them, and turn out each jelly onto the plate.

Spoon the fruits equally onto each plate. Cut the strawberries and remaining passion fruits in half. Place half a passion fruit next to each jelly, then scatter over the strawberry halves.

Lastly, sprinkle over a few paw paw seeds. You could add a sprig of mint, one of the few times that I think it's justified. And serve.

MANGO MOUSSE WITH MANGO SAUCE

This is a basic recipe for mousse, and you could use raspberries, apricots, brambles, passion fruit or (if they're sweet and ripe) strawberries. It keeps for up to 48 hours.

5 leaves gelatine, soaked in cold
   water for 15 minutes
6 large ripe, mangoes
200 g (7 oz) sugar
125 ml (4¼ fl oz) egg whites
450 ml (15 fl oz) double cream
8 × No. 1 dariole moulds (or
   ramekins)

SERVES EIGHT

Skin the mangoes and hack away the flesh from the stones. Put the flesh into a liquidiser (this is best done in two batches) and whizz them until you have a nice, smooth purée. Pass this through a sieve, measure out 600 ml (20 fl oz) of purée and put it to one side.

Dissolve the sugar in a little water over a high heat and boil the resulting syrup down to the softball stage (see Armagnac Parfait on page 135). Remove it from the heat.

Whisk the egg whites and, when they start to thicken up, slowly pour on the softball sugar syrup. Continue to whisk for three further minutes.

Remove the gelatine leaves from the cold water and squeeze them dry. In a medium-sized saucepan, warm the mango purée through (do not let it boil!) and dissolve the gelatine in it.

Pour the purée and gelatine mix onto the meringue and fold it in until fully incorporated. Now whisk the cream into a soft peak and fold it into the meringue mix. This is your mousse. Pour it into a large jug – this makes it easier to then pour it into the individual moulds.

Leave to chill overnight in the fridge.

To serve, dip the moulds in hot water for 15 to 20 seconds, then turn them out onto chilled plates. Spoon the remaining mango purée around them. Serve.

PART ELEVEN

BASIC RECIPES

STOCKS AND SAUCES – AN INTRODUCTION

Good stocks, and therefore good sauces, lift your meals into a different league. When you are making the sauce for your dish, the only surefire way to become a culinary hero is by using home-made stock. Stock cube, and the slightly better ready-made stocks available from supermarkets, will do the job for you, but it's not the same. So, be a hero and read these tips:

Always make stocks whenever you have free time. That way, you can freeze them until they're needed.

Don't try to make stock a few hours before your dinner party – it will end in tears.

Unless you are reducing a stock to thicken it, avoid fast boiling. This will cause emulsification and make it cloudy.

With the exception of Nage (see page 160), always try to cool your stock quickly and leave it overnight in the fridge. This allows the fat to solidify on the surface and the sediment to settle on the bottom, making it easier to extract the pure, clear stock.

It pays to cultivate your local fishmonger or butcher, so that you can obtain a regular supply of fish, chicken or beef bones for your stocks. Give them a bit of warning and they'll keep them by for you.

That's it. The difference home-made stocks make to your cooking will ensure that stock cubes become a last resort.

NAGE (MARINATED VEGETABLE STOCK)

This stock is essential to the making of Nage Butter Sauce, which will crop up regularly throughout this book, so make big batches of this when you can. It freezes well and the ingredients are always reasonably easy to get. Freeze it in 600 ml (1 pint) tubs, and defrost when you need it.

1 large onion
1 leek
2 sticks of celery
1 bulb fennel (optional)
4 large carrots
1 head of garlic, sliced in half across its equator
8 white peppercorns, crushed
1 teaspoon pink peppercorns
1 teaspoon coriander seeds
1 star anise
1 bay leaf
40 g (1½ oz) mixed fresh herbs
300 ml (10 fl oz) white wine

Chop all of the vegetables into 1-cm (½-in) dice, place in a pot and cover with water. Add the garlic, peppercorns, coriander seeds, star anise and bay leaf, bring to the boil and simmer for eight minutes. Add the fresh herbs and simmer for a further three minutes. Now add the white wine and remove from the heat. Leave covered and allow to marinate for 48 hours in a cool place.

Once marinated, strain the stock through a fine sieve. It can be used immediately or be frozen for up to six weeks.

MAKES 1.2 LITRES
(2 PINTS)

FISH AND CHICKEN STOCK – AN INTRODUCTION

Good fish and chicken stock should form a slight jelly consistency. When cutting garlic for stock, always cut whole garlic heads across their 'equators'. This gives you solely the sweet garlic flavours and not the harsh, garlic oil.

In the summer, it's best to freeze the stock immediately but in the winter, it will keep for up to 48 hours in the fridge. You can make bigger batches by multiplying the ingredients up to any number, dependant on the largest stock pot you have. I find that the bigger the batch the better the stock!

FISH STOCK

Soak the fish bones in the cold water for half an hour. Drain, wash and roughly chop.

In a medium-sized saucepan, gently sweat all of the finely diced vegetables, peppercorns, bay leaf and herbs in the olive oil until soft, but without colouring them. Add the white wine and boil until nearly dry. Now add the fishbones and stir to coat. Pour over enough cold water to just cover the mixture. Bring it to the boil, skim and then simmer for about 18 minutes. (Do *not* allow it to boil.) Remove it from the heat and allow to stand until cool (this takes about three to four hours).

Once cooled, pour the stock through a sieve or colander, then pass it through a fine sieve into a tall container. Place in the fridge and leave it overnight to allow the stock to settle.

The next day, skim off any scum that has settled on the top, then spoon off all of the clear jellied stock which should then be frozen until needed.

You may notice some white gunge at the bottom of the container – urg. This should not be considered edible and should be disposed of in a humane fashion.

750 g (1½ lb) fish bones, preferably sole, turbot, or brill
1 litre (2 pints) cold water
½ medium-sized onion, finely diced
1 white of leek, finely diced
1 stick of celery, finely diced
15 g (½ oz) fresh herbs, try chervil, parsley, tarragon and coriander
6 white peppercorns
½ bay leaf
1 tablespoon olive oil
300 ml (10 fl oz) dry white wine

**MAKES 300 ML
(10 FL OZ)**

CHICKEN STOCK

3 chicken carcasses, skins and fat
 removed
1 large carrot, quartered
2 medium leeks
2 sticks of celery, halved lengthwise
1 onion with skin left on, quartered
1 small bulb garlic, halved across its
 equator
6 white peppercorns
1 bay leaf
1 sprig of thyme
15 g (½ oz) parsley or tarragon
 stalks

MAKES 1.4 LITRES
(2¼ PINTS)

Place the carcasses into a pot large enough for the bones to take up half its depth. *Just* cover them with about 2.5 litres (4 pints) of cold water (too much water and you'll end up diluting it) and bring to boil.

Once boiling, skim off the fat and any scum from the surface. Add the rest of the ingredients, all of which should lie on top of the carcasses. Adjust heat to a simmer and skim once more.

The simmering stock will now rise and fall through the vegetables, which acts as a filter, absorbing all of the gunk from the liquid and leaving it crystal clear.

Leave it to simmer like this for three to four hours, tasting regularly. You should eventually notice the point at which the flavour stops improving. This means it's ready.

Remove the pan from heat and empty the stock into a colander set over a bowl. Now pass the stock through a fine sieve into a tall container or 2.25 litre (4 pint) jug. Cover it and allow it to cool by placing it into a sink of cold water.

When it's cool, place it in fridge overnight until any fat settles on top. Skim off the fat and spoon out the now jellied stock into tubs and freeze until ready to use.

BEEF STOCK

Making beef stock is messy and time consuming (it has to be simmered for eight hours) and is only really necessary for 'Jus' sauces – *i.e.* those sauces which are just the reduction of a stock, needing the 'body' of a beef stock to prevent them from becoming watery.

Usually, I just add a little cream and butter to my sauces to achieve this. Some sauces, however, really need a bit of beef stock.

Pre-heat the oven to 200°C/400°F/Gas Mark 6.

Place the beef knuckle bones into a large roasting tray. Put it into the hot oven for approximately one hour until it is well browned. Tip off the liquid marrow fat and reserve.

Heat a large stockpot until very hot and add three tablespoons of the marrow fat (which should smoke as soon as it hits the pan). Add all the vegetables (apart from the tomatoes), the herbs, bay leaf and peppercorns. Stir thoroughly on a high heat until well browned – it is important to achieve a good colour without burning.

When a good, dark colour has been achieved, add the tomatoes and tomato purée and stir frequently until the tomatoes are cooked to a pulp.

Add the wine and reduce it until just dry. Now add the beef bones, the pig's trotter and the shin of beef and cover with cold water. Bring to the boil, skimming the surface all the time, then reduce the heat until the surface barely trembles and allow everything to simmer for at least eight hours or preferably overnight.

When you wake up, get into the kitchen to pass off the liquid. I tip the contents into a large colander set over another pot. Allow the stock to cool. Once cold, skim off any fat and pour the liquid through a fine sieve into 600 ml (1 pint) tubs and freeze the stock until it's needed.

4.5 kg (10 lb) of beef knuckle bones
1 pig's trotter
900 g (2 lb) shin of beef
2 large carrots, cut into 2.5 cm (1 in) lengths
2 large onions, each cut into 8 wedges
2 large leeks, cut into 2.5 cm (1 in) lengths
2 sticks of celery, cut to 2.5 cm (1 in) lengths
1 head of garlic, halved across its equator
15 g (½ oz) parsley or tarragon stalks
1 bay leaf
1 large sprig of thyme
12 whole black peppercorns
3 plum tomatoes, quartered
2 tablespoons tomato purée
300 ml (10 fl oz) red wine

MAKES 1.2 LITRES (2 PINTS)

NAGE BUTTER SAUCE

This sauce is my own favourite and the one I use most in my cooking. It is a delightful, fresh, buttery sauce on its own, but with the addition of other ingredients (freshly chopped herbs, chilli, pesto, tomato, shellfish . . . you name it) it can become anything you desire.

It is easy to make, and the base ingredients are easily obtainable. The one item of equipment which is essential in the making of this sauce though, is a hand-held blender. Without one, it is difficult to obtain the light, smooth quality which makes it so versatile.

A word on 'splitting'. This is an emulsion sauce (a combination of fat and liquid), so if you don't give it sufficient heat and keep it moving, then it will split — *i.e.* you will end up with big globs of butter floating on the top — not dissimilar to a commercial Salad Dressing.

600 ml (1 pint) Nage Vegetable
  Stock (see page 160)
200 g (7 oz) unsalted butter, cold
  and diced
1 teaspoon lemon juice
Pinch of salt
4 turns of white pepper

**MAKES APPROX. 300 ML
(10 FL OZ)**

Pour the Nage Vegetable Stock into a small, straight-sided saucepan, filling slightly more than half the pan. Place on a high heat and bring to the boil. Reduce down to roughly one fifth of the original volume. (It turns dark and looks thick and sticky!).

Turn the heat to low and plop in all of the butter. Stick in your hand-held blender or put it in an electric mixer and give it a good old thrash about until all of the butter has been melted and the texture is light and frothy.

Add the lemon juice, salt and pepper, tasting as you season and keep warm (but don't let it boil) until it's needed.

If you let this sauce go cold and it solidifies, you can bring it back again by melting the sauce. It will 'split' — *i.e.* the butter will float to the top. Now boil 85 ml (3 fl oz) of double cream in a small saucepan. When it's boiling, use the hand blender to whisk it and, at the same time, pour the hot split sauce into the saucepan in a steady stream. And hey presto, lovely light sauce.

DUCK FAT

Not so much a recipe as a technique. Duck fat is rendered duck skin (*i.e.* boiled down until the fat is released). It's a bit of a hassle to prepare, but it does impart a unique flavour to whatever is cooked with it. There is no substitute for the taste, but Clarified Butter (see page 175) will do the job. There are two ways to get your duck fat; the first is to follow the directions below. The second is to buy it in a tin from a specialist delicatessen.

Remove the breasts and legs (retain for cooking). Strip off the skin from the duck carcasses. Voilà, duckskin! Keep the carcasses for stock.

Place all the duck skin into a medium-sized saucepan and add the thyme, bay leaf and garlic. Pour over just enough cold water to cover, put the pan onto the stove and bring to the boil.

Reduce the heat to very low and leave for two to three hours, until all the water has boiled away and the fat has melted.

Strain the fat off through a fine sieve into a container and store in the fridge until needed.

This will keep for six weeks.

3 whole ducks
1 sprig thyme
1 bay leaf
1 head of garlic, halved across its equator

MAKES ABOUT 300 ML (10 FL OZ)

HOME DRIED TOMATOES

These are a sweet and plump version of what usually comes in jars labelled 'Sun Dried Tomatoes' and which, in my opinion, look and taste like shoe leather. Forego the supermarket chains and make 'em yourself – it's worth it. But beware! It *is* important to obtain really good, ripe plum tomatoes – the little Dutch waterballs won't work!

Approximately twelve hours of oven time is involved in the making of these, so don't plan on using your oven for anything else today. Better still, you can do them overnight. It's worth it – they *are* a taste sensation.

12 large, ripe plum tomatoes

Maldon salt

Fresh ground white pepper

50 ml (2 fl oz) olive oil plus extra for preserving (approx. 200 ml [7 fl oz] for a 300 ml [1-pint] kilner jar)

1 sprig basil or thyme

1 clove of garlic, crushed

**MAKES 24
HOME DRIED TOMATOES**

Pre-heat the oven to 110°C/225°F/Gas Mark ¼.

Slice the tomatoes in half, through the growing eye at the top. Then remove the green eye. Lay the tomatoes on a baking sheet, cut side up, and sprinkle lightly with crushed Maldon salt and 12 turns of pepper. Drizzle the olive oil over them.

Place the tomatoes into the oven (some of you may have to prop the oven door open slightly to keep the temperature down). Leave for eight hours.

When you return, the tomatoes should be reduced to half their original side but *not* browned. Turn them over and leave for a further four hours or until they are nice and firm.

Remove from the oven and leave until cool. Then place them in a kilner jar and add a sprig of fresh basil or thyme, the crushed clove of garlic and then cover in olive oil. These ultra tasty beauties can now be stored in your fridge for up to three weeks.

I realise that this takes a fair bit of time to do, but it *is* worth it. The only way you'll find out is if you try it . . .

PESTO

The traditional version of this sauce uses only basil leaves. I like to vary it by using a combination of flat leaf parsley, rocket and basil. You can double the amount of olive oil to make a runny pesto which looks good drizzled onto the plate.

Place all the ingredients in a food processor and whizz for 30 seconds. Scrape around inside with a plastic spatula and whizz again for a further 30 seconds. That's it.

Scoop out into a kilner or screwtop jar. It may be stored in the fridge for up to two weeks. Each time you've used some of it, you should flatten down the surface with a broad spoon and then splash on some more olive oil before returning it to the fridge. This keeps it sealed, and stops it darkening and losing its flavour.

75 g (3 oz) basil, flat leaf parsley, rocket leaves
50 g (2 oz) fresh Parmesan, grated
50 g (2 oz) pine nut kernels
2 cloves garlic, peeled and roughly chopped
1 teaspoon Maldon salt
12 turns fresh ground white pepper
200 ml (6 fl oz) of virgin olive oil

**MAKES APPROX.
A 450-ML
(15-FL OZ) JAR**

TAPENADE

This is a classic Provençal olive, caper and anchovy sauce – great on toast, pizzas, roast courgettes, aubergines and fennel. The tuna in my version helps to make it milder and I love it dolloped onto fresh tomato soup.

50 g (2 oz) tinned anchovy fillets, drained

2 cloves of garlic

175 g (6 oz) black olives, pitted

50 g (2 oz) tinned tuna in oil, drained

50 g (2 oz) capers (dry and salted rather than in brine – wash them first)

Juice of ½ lemon

1 sprig thyme, leaves removed and stalk discarded

1 bay leaf

120 ml (4 fl oz) olive oil

1 tablespoon brandy

Place *all* the ingredients into a food processor and whizz it up for about two minutes. Scrape the result into a kilner jar or sealable, airtight tub.

This will keep for four weeks in your fridge.

**MAKES APPROX.
A 450-ML
(15-FL OZ) JAR**

CHILLI OIL

WARNING! This stuff is mega, mega spicy and you'll have to take care not to get any in your eyes or other sensitive parts. Used sparingly, chilli oil imparts a wonderful glow to many dishes.

(SAFETY TIP – don't fry anything with it).

Slice the chillies in half, lengthwise, and place in a saucepan. Pour on the oil, plonk it on your hob and bring to the boil. Simmer gently for five minutes, remove from the heat and allow to cool. (This takes approximately two hours.)

Once cooled, transfer the chillis and oil to a plastic tub with a lid and store in a cool place for two to three weeks. Then, pour the oil through a sieve to remove the chillies before using it (or else your oil will just get too hot).

I usually keep the chilli oil in an old olive oil bottle, but remember to label it well. A skull and crossbones will suffice.

225 g (8 oz) ripe, red chillies
1 litre (2 pints) sunflower oil

MAKES APPROX. 1 LITRE (2 PINTS)

VINAIGRETTE

This is my version of the classic French salad dressing. It has evolved over the years into this present form – a bit of an 'everything but the kitchen sink' recipe, but well worth trying. After all, ten years of research and development must count for something.

1 tablespoon smooth Dijon
  mustard
100 ml (3½ fl oz) white wine
  vinegar
100 ml (3½ fl oz) balsamic vinegar
200 ml (7 fl oz) hazelnut oil
200 ml (7 fl oz) sunflower oil
200 ml (7 fl oz) olive oil
1 teaspoon salt
12 turns white pepper
1 clove garlic, peeled and crushed

**MAKES APPROX.
750 ML (1¼ PINTS)**

Place all the ingredients into a liquidiser and blitz them for 60 seconds. Strain the result through a fine sieve into a jug, from which you can pour the vinaigrette into any container of your choosing. Personally, I keep mine in an old olive oil bottle, which means that I can give it a good shake before using. A well rinsed out detergent bottle is also good.

TOMATOES CONCASSE

Skinned, de-seeded and with the acidic water removed, these small sweet cubes of tomato can be used for sauces and salads. Like everything else, the success of even such a basic preparation depends on the use of the best quality ingredients.

Remove the skins from the tomatoes. To do this, you can either.

a) Slit a wee cross at the bottom of the tomatoes with a sharp knife. Pop them into boiling water and leave for a minute before removing with a draining spoon. The skin should peel off easily.

or (my preferred method)

b) Use a blowtorch. First, spear one of your tomatoes with the tip of a sharp knife. Light your blowtorch and apply the flame to the tomato skin, moving on as the skin blisters. Same effect as (a), but much more fun.

Once peeled, cut the tomatoes into quarters, scoop out the seeds and set aside then cut the flesh into a 5-mm (¼-in) dice. That's it. Tomatoes Concasse. Best used immediately, but they will keep for a maximum of 24 hours. (Keep and freeze the tomato pulp, seeds and water, for use in stocks and sauces.)

Ripe, plum tomatoes
(minimum quantity – 1)

PASTA DOUGH

Fresh pasta lifts your cooking into the gourmet class, so it's worth learning how to make it. At the restaurant, we use imported French flour (T55), but this is only marginally better than good old ordinary plain flour.

Pasta dough is simple to make, although you WILL require a pasta machine.

150 g (5 oz) plain flour
1 whole egg, size 3
1 egg yolk, size 3

MAKES ABOUT EIGHT SERVINGS

Place the flour into a food processor and start giving it a whizz round. Add the whole egg and egg yolk and keep whizzing until the mixture resembles fine breadcrumbs (it shouldn't be dusty, nor should it be a big, gooey ball). This takes two to three minutes.

Tip out the dough and form into a ball shape. Knead it briskly for one minute. Wrap in clingfilm and place it in the fridge for one hour before using.

Now cut the dough into two pieces. For each piece, flatten with a rolling pin to 5 mm (¼ in) thickness. Fold over the dough and roll it out, re-folding and rolling seven times until you have a rectangular shape 7.5 × 18 cm (3 × 7 in). It is important to work the dough until it is nice and shiny, as this gives it the *al dente* texture.

With the pasta machine at its widest setting, pass the dough through the rollers. Repeat this process, decreasing the roller setting down grade by grade with each pass. For most uses, I take the pasta down to the penultimate setting.

Once the desired thickness is reached, pass the dough through a second time at the same setting, then allow it to dry for about five minutes. Hanging it is the best way to dry the pasta and at Braeval, I use a suspended broomhandle, but for smaller quantities, use the handle of a wooden spoon (the end weighed down with a heavy book), being careful not to poke yourself in the eye with the handle.

For lasagne, cut the pasta dough into squares (or rounds, if you prefer). For fettucine, pass the dough through the machine's big cutters. For tagliatelle, pass through the small cutters.

WORDS OF WARNING:
Do *not* add salt to the pasta dough. This only toughens it.
Do *not* add oil to the cooking water. It will *not* prevent sticking and is therefore a complete waste of oil.
Do *not* dredge the pasta in flour to prevent sticking, as the flour turns to glue when cooked and, ironically, causes the pasta to stick.

To cook the pasta have a large pot of boiling, salted water ready. Drop in the pasta, stirring until it comes back to the boil again. Cook for two and a half minutes, then remove with a slotted spoon or spaghetti fork and cool in a bowl of cold water. Drain thoroughly and, if not using immediately, store in a tub for up to 12 hours before use. Once stored, the pasta will stick together. To unstick, add some water, swirl around and drain again.

BREADCRUMBS

The *best* use for stale bread (apart from feeding ducks).

Remove the crusts from slices of stale bread and place the slices into a food processor. Whizz them until you have fine breadcrumbs. It is best to do this in small batches.

I quantity of stale white bread

Spread the breadcrumbs on a wide tray and leave in a warm place for 12 hours.

Stored in an airtight container until needed they will keep for up to two weeks.

ROASTED RED PEPPERS

Like the Duck Fat preparation, this is more of a technique than a recipe. Look for nice, large, ripe red peppers (they should feel heavy when picked up). The secret here is to get the skin of the pepper totally blackened without burning the flesh underneath.

6 red peppers
Olive oil for preserving
1 clove garlic
1 sprig thyme
1 bay leaf

There are three ways to do this:

GRILLING: Turn the grill on to high. Drizzle a little olive oil over the peppers and place them under the grill, turning as the skin blackens.

BAKING: Pre-heat the oven to 240°C/475°F/Gas Mark 9. Place the peppers in a shallow baking tray in the top part of the oven. Turn as they blacken.

SKEWERED OVER A GAS BURNER: My favoured method. Prong the peppers on a skewer and place directly over a burner on a gas cooker, turning as they blacken. I personally use a blowtorch to finish off any little hard-to-get patches of red.

Once the skin is totally blackened, wrap the peppers in clingfilm and allow to cool. Unwrap them and wash off the blackened skin with water. Slice the peppers into quarters. Remove and discard the pith and seeds from inside.

Use the peppers straight away or store by placing them in a kilner jar, pouring in enough olive oil to cover them. Add the garlic clove, thyme and bay leaf for flavour. They will keep for up to two weeks in the fridge.

OLIVE OIL CROÛTONS

These are terrific in soups or scattered over salads to give a crunchy texture. A word of caution however – *don't* be tempted to nibble at these. Once you start, you won't stop and you'll end up having to make more. They are extremely addictive – you have been warned!

Remove and discard the crusts from the bread. Cut the bread into 5 mm (¼ in) squares.

Warm a frying pan through (but not too hot). Add the olive oil and crushed garlic. Allow to infuse on a low heat for about five minutes.

Drop the cubes of bread into the pan and fry gently, stirring from time to time with a wooden spoon. After 10–15 minutes the Croûtons should be golden brown. Add the seasoning before removing the Croûtons from pan and allow to drain on absorbent kitchen roll. Discard the garlic.

Keep warm until ready to use or store in an airtight container for up to 24 hours.

4 slices of bread, 5 mm (¼ in) thick, cubed
85 ml (3 fl oz) olive oil
1 clove garlic, lightly crushed
Pinch Maldon salt
3 turns fresh ground white pepper

MAKES SIX TO TWELVE PORTIONS, DEPENDING ON APPETITES

CLARIFIED BUTTER

Clarified butter is just the oily part of butter, *i.e.* without the buttermilk, and is essential for frying Rosti Potatoes (see page 128), to give them a rich, buttery flavour. You could buy it ready prepared in Indian delicatessens (they call it *Ghee*) and it can also be used in place of duck fat.

In a small saucepan, melt the butter on a low heat. Allow it to stand for a few minutes until all the oil rises to the top, then skim off the oil into a sealable plastic container. It will keep for two months. If you have a microwave, put the butter in a plastic jug and microwave on a high heat for one minute. If it is not completely melted, heat again for a further 30 seconds. Do not allow it to boil and continue as above. Discard the watery buttermilk.

250 g (9 oz) unsalted butter

MAKES APPROX. 200 ML (7 FL OZ)

OLIVE OIL SAUCES – AN INTRODUCTION

I use two similar olive oil sauces. One has a Mediterranean flavour whilst the other is oriental in style. They both tend to be lumped under the title of Sauce Vierge because they both use virgin olive oil. To avoid confusion, I'll call them Mediterranean Sauce Vierge and Oriental Sauce Vierge.

They're both dead easy to make, but take note: The Mediterranean version keeps for up to two weeks, but the Oriental version has to be used the same day it's made.

Use the best oil you can get – good virgin olive oil is very important here.

MEDITERRANEAN SAUCE VIERGE

200 ml (7 fl oz) extra virgin olive oil

100 g (4 oz) shallots, finely chopped

1 clove garlic, lightly crushed but still whole

1 sprig thyme

1 bay leaf

25 ml (1 fl oz) sherry vinegar

1 teaspoon Maldon salt, crushed

12 turns fresh ground white pepper

MAKES APPROX. 175 ML (6 FL OZ)

Place all the ingredients, except for the vinegar, in a small pan. Warm it through on a gentle heat until the sauce is hot, but not boiling – you want to soften those shallots, but not colour them. Heat this way for 20 minutes.

Remove from the heat, add the sherry vinegar and allow to cool. Once cooled, remove the bay leaf, thyme and crushed garlic clove.

This keeps for up to two weeks in the fridge, to be reheated when required. The sauce is also excellent cold, however and I particularly like it with some Pesto and Tomatoes Concasse mixed through it before serving.

ORIENTAL SAUCE VIERGE

The Japanese pickled ginger in this recipe is a rather lurid pink and is traditionally a garnish for sushi. I love its sweet, sharp flavour. You can get it in most Chinese supermarkets.

In a small pan, combine the olive oil and the crushed coriander seeds. Heat until just simmering, then remove from the heat and allow to infuse for five minutes.

Pour in the lemon juice and the remaining ingredients and keep warm until ready to serve. Personally I don't like leaving it for more than 30 minutes.

Stir well before serving. It will split slightly on the plate, but this is fine.

85 ml (3 fl oz) extra virgin olive oil
5 g (1 teaspoon) coriander seeds, crushed
25 ml (1 fl oz) lemon juice
1 tablespoon coriander leaves, finely shredded
2 slices (1 teaspoon) Japanese pickled ginger, finely chopped

MAKES ABOUT 120 ML (4 FL OZ)

STOCK SYRUP

Used in desserts, this is a 50/50 mix of sugar and water. It keeps for eight weeks in the fridge, so make it well in advance and you'll always have it handy. It's good for poaching fruit and can be flavoured with cinnamon, vanilla, lemon, orange – you name it!

1 kg (2¼ lb) granulated sugar
1 litre (1¾ pints)

**MAKES 1.4 LITRES
(2¼ PINTS)**

Put the sugar with the water in a medium-size saucepan, place on a high heat and bring to the boil, stirring from time to time.

Simmer for five minutes before skimming off any impurities which may have risen to the surface. Leave to cool.

And that, as they say, is that.

PART TWELVE

MISCELLANEOUS RECIPES

BREADMAKING – AN INTRODUCTION

Breadmaking can be a therapeutic experience – creating a loaf of fine smelling, hot, fresh bread is just so satisfying. One of the secrets of good bread is in the kneading, and you should endeavour to keep a nice smooth outside skin on the dough as you work it. Do this, and the dough will rise evenly.

The six most common mistakes are:

Too much water: sticky dough.
Too little water: hard lumpy dough.
Too cold proving: dough won't rise.
Too hot proving: dough rises, then dies.
Too much salt: kills the yeast (so it doesn't rise)
Too little kneading: heavy bread.
Too much kneading: heavy bread.

Breadmaking is a case of practice makes perfect, so go for it.

BRAEVAL BREAD

Dried yeast could be used here, but doesn't give quite as good a result. Fresh yeast is available from some bakers – but you'll probably have to give them 24 hours notice.

900 g (2 lb) strong plain flour
50 g (2 oz) unsalted butter
3 teaspoons salt, level
25 g (1 oz) fresh yeast
1 teaspoon caster sugar, heaped
450 ml (15 fl oz) warm water

YOU WILL ALSO NEED:

4 × 750 g (1½ lb) loaf tins
1 electric mixer & dough hook (or
  strong hands!)
1 large mixing bowl
Clingfilm
A damp tea towel
A baking sheet and cooling rack

MAKES FOUR 750 G (1½ LB) LOAVES

Pre-heat the oven to 200°C/400°F/Gas Mark 6.

Place the flour, butter and salt in a bowl of the electric food mixer. Work in the ingredients with your hands until you have dispersed the butter. Dissolve the yeast and sugar in the warm water and add it to the bowl. Mix everything with the dough hook running at a slow to medium speed. Once fully incorporated, set the machine to a slow speed and leave it to work the dough for a full 10 minutes. The dough should then come cleanly away from the sides of the bowl. You could do this by hand, it just takes a bit of elbow grease.

Tip the dough out onto a lightly floured surface and work it with your hands until you feel the dough 'tighten' (this should occur after approximately five minutes).

Place the dough into a large, lightly oiled, metal bowl and cover it with clingfilm or a damp tea towel. Put the bowl in a warm place and leave it to prove until the dough has risen out of the top of the bowl, approximately doubling in volume. This takes between 30 and 60 minutes.

Tip the dough out onto a worktop, give it a quick knead by hand and then form it into a smooth ball. Cut the dough into quarters and form each one into a loaf shape, then drop them into the lightly oiled 750 g (1½ lb) loaf tins.

Place these in a warm place and cover them with the damp tea towel – this prevents a skin forming (which would not allow an even rise on the loaf).

Wait until the loaves are well risen (just over the top of the tin) before removing the towel and leave them for up to five minutes before placing the tins on a baking tray in the oven. Be careful not to knock the tins, as at this stage the dough is very light and well risen and could fall, giving you a squashed loaf.

Bake the loaves for 15 minutes, then carefully remove them from the tins. Place them side down on the tray and cook for a further 10 minutes. Remove the tray from the oven, turn the loaves over and put them back to bake for a further 10–15 minutes.

The loaves are ready when they are a deep brown colour and sound hollow when tapped. Leave them to cool on a rack.

You can either use the bread that day, or wrap the loaves individually in clingfilm as soon as they're cool and freeze. They will keep for three weeks.

To regenerate the loaves from frozen, place each loaf, still in clingfilm, in a microwave and cook it on the highest setting for two minutes. Allow the loaf to stand for eight minutes before removing the clingfilm.

Alternatively, allow the loaves to stand at room temperature for about four hours.

OLIVE OIL BREAD

This loaf uses olive oil instead of butter, and I prefer it not to be cooked in a tin – just rounded by hand into a loaf shape and cooked on a baking sheet. This gives it a thicker crust and has the added advantage of being less fiddly to do.

Because there is more exposed crust, you need to keep the loaves moist. Do this by spraying the damp tea towel a couple of times with a plant sprayer filled with warm water whilst the bread is proving.

It also improves the crust if you bung an ovenproof dish of hot water into the bottom of the oven to keep the atmosphere humid.

CLOCKWISE FROM TOP LEFT: Olive Oil Bread (page 181); Walnut, Apricot and Raisin Bread (page 185); Brioche (page 187); Olive Oil Bread (as before) and Braeval Bread (page 180).

1.25 kg (2½ lb) strong plain flour
120 ml (4 fl oz) olive oil
500 ml (17 fl oz) warm water
40 g (1½ oz) fresh yeast
12 g (2 teaspoons) sugar
20 g (3 teaspoons) salt

MAKES FOUR LOAVES

Pre-heat the oven to 230°C/450°F/Gas Mark 8.

Place the flour and olive oil into the bowl of your food mixer. Fit the dough hook and switch it on to a medium speed.

Dissolve the yeast and sugar in the warm water and slowly pour it onto the mixing flour. After a minute or so, the flour should come together to form a dough. Reduce the speed to a slow to medium speed and knead for a further eight minutes.

Add the salt and knead for another two minutes. Then tip the dough out onto a lightly-floured surface and hand knead it for three to four minutes until you feel the dough tighten. Pop the dough into a large, oiled mixing bowl (you could clean and use the bowl from the electric mixer) and cover it with a damp tea towel. Put it in a warm place and allow it to prove until it has doubled in size (it will take about 35 minutes), using the plant spray every so often to keep the tea towel moist.

Tip the proven dough out onto a floured surface and gently knead it for two minutes. Form the dough into a large ball and then, using a sharp knife, cut it into quarters. Form each quarter into a smooth ball, getting them as near as possible into a spherical shape.

Place the loaves onto a lightly-floured baking sheet, cover with a damp tea towel and put them back in the warm place to prove for a further 30 minutes. Ten minutes before you bake the bread put an ovenproof dish of water in the bottom of the oven.

When doubled in size, remove the towel and give the loaves a quick squirt with the plant spray and bake them for 20 minutes in the warm oven.

When they are ready, the loaves should be well fired on top (very dark brown). Remove them from oven and place them on a cooling rack.

You may scoff them as soon as they're cooled or cover in clingfilm and freeze until required. Defrost as described in Braeval Bread (see page 180).

WALNUT, APRICOT AND RAISIN BREAD

Easy to make and great with cheese . . .

Pre-heat the oven to 230°C/450°F/Gas Mark 8.

Dissolve the yeast in the water and place it into a mixing bowl. Add the oil and flour and bring together to form a dough. Remove it from bowl with your hands and knead it for seven minutes. Add the walnuts, apricots, raisins and salt and work it for a further three minutes.

Cut the dough into six pieces and roll it into sausage shapes about 12 cm (5 in) long and 5 cm (2 in) wide. Place them onto a floured baking sheet, cover them with a damp teatowel and allow them to prove for 30 minutes in a warm place until doubled in size – don't worry if the rolls join together.

Place the tray of water in the bottom of the pre-heated oven. Leave it for ten minutes. The water will start to steam, making the air in the oven moist, which will help the bread to rise and give it a nice, crisp crust.

Place the loaves into the middle of the oven for 25–30 minutes. It should be golden brown on the top when ready and should sound hollow when tapped on the bottom.

Remove the loaves and leave them on a rack to cool. Dust each one with flour and eat immediately or wrap them individually in clingfilm and freeze.

To regenerate the loaves from frozen refer to Braeval Bread on page 180.

25 g (1 oz) fresh yeast
600 ml (20 fl oz) warm water
50 ml (2 fl oz) olive oil
1 kg (2¼ lb) strong, plain flour
50 ml (2 fl oz) walnut oil
25 g (1 oz) salt
200 g (7 oz) combination of walnuts, diced dried apricots and raisins (I use a 3, 2, 2 ratio)

YOU WILL ALSO NEED:
1 baking sheet
1 large mixing bowl
A damp tea towel
A cooling rack
A tray half-filled with water

MAKES SIX LOAVES

BRAEVAL TABLET

This is a traditional Scottish sweetie and it's like a hard, crumbly fudge. Very sweet, but beloved by anyone who's ever had it. Me, in particular.

I've always been very vague about this recipe whenever asked, since it took me a *long* time to perfect it, but some things just shouldn't be kept to oneself. I must warn you, however, if you don't know already, that tablet is *very addictive* and should be kept out of the way of children and adults alike. They'd only go and eat it and there'd be less for you.

1 × 30 cm × 24 cm (12 in × 8 in) baking tin, lined with greaseproof paper
400 ml (14 fl oz) tin of condensed milk
1 kg (2¼ lb) granulated sugar
250 g (9 oz) unsalted butter
600 ml (20 fl oz) hot water
25 g (1 oz) grated white chocolate (optional, but recommended)

Place all the ingredients into a large saucepan and bring them to the boil before reducing to a medium heat. *This temperature is all important!* Too cold and the tablet will turn dark brown but won't set. Too hot and the tablet will burn on the bottom. The temperature is about right when the tablet is simmering at about double its original volume.

Simmer for 30–40 minutes until the tablet has darkened to a golden caramel and started to thicken. Give it a stir at this stage. It will probably have 'caught' a bit at the bottom of the pan, but worry not – this is normal and the bits are dispersed during the beating later.

Now remove the pan from the heat and add the white chocolate if you are using it. Apart from adding extra flavour, it helps the tablet to set.

Start beating the mixture with a wooden spoon or electric mixer and don't stop until it starts to thicken and set in the pan. It takes about ten minutes.

Pour it into the lined tray and allow it to set for 10 to 15 minutes. Then, using a thin bladed knife, cut the tablet into 1 cm (½ in) squares. Leave it for two to three hours to harden.

Remove the tablet from tray, breaking it into the squares and store it in an airtight container. Tablet stales after four to five days, but I don't expect it will survive that long once you've started dishing it out.

NB. I now use an electric hand whisk instead of a wooden spoon. It isn't any faster, but it saves you a sore arm. I'd have told you earlier, but I don't see why you should get *everything* handed to you on a plate.

BRIOCHE

A wickedly rich buttery loaf, much beloved of the French and the best partner to strawberry jam I know. I find it slightly less temperamental than bread and even 'not so brilliant' brioche tastes great!

Pre-heat the oven to 200°C/400°F/Gas Mark 6.

In the mixer bowl, dissolve the yeast and sugar in the warm milk, then whisk in the eggs. Fit the dough hook and mix it on a medium to high speed, slowly adding the flour, a spoonful at a time. As the dough starts to thicken, turn the speed back to medium and then a low to medium speed.

Add the salt and work the dough for seven to eight minutes until it's firm. Then add the soft butter a piece at a time, kneading again until fully incorporated. Once incorporated, knead for a further five to six minutes until the dough is shiny and elastic.

Remove the dough to a floured worktop and work by hand until you feel the dough 'tighten'. This will take about two to three minutes.

Form the dough into a ball and return it to the mixer bowl. Cover the bowl with clingfilm and leave it in a warm place to prove for about 40 minutes until doubled in size.

When the dough has doubled in size, tip it out onto a floured worktop and lightly knead it for one minute. Form the dough into a large, shiny ball and

120 ml (4 fl oz) warm milk
60 g (2 oz) yeast
60 g (2 oz) sugar
8 eggs
1 kg (2¼ lb) strong plain flour
3 teaspoons salt, heaped
350 g (12 oz) unsalted butter,
  softened to room temperature

YOU WILL ALSO NEED:
Electric mixer
4 x 450 g (1 lb) oiled bread tins
Baking tray
A damp teatowel
Clingfilm

cut it into quarters. Roll each quarter into a ball and then form it into a loaf shape.

Place the loaves into the oiled tins on a baking sheet and cover them with the damp teatowel. Put them in a warm place and leave it until the dough has risen out of the tins.

Remove the towel and prove the dough until it is fully risen. In total this will take 45 minutes. A good place to do this is on top of the stove, since your oven will already be pre-heating. The brioche should rise about 2.5 cm (1 in) out of the tins.

Place the brioche in the pre-heated oven for 15 minutes, then remove them from the tins and cook for a further eight minutes on each side (*i.e.* a total cooking time of 31 minutes). Remove them from oven and cool the brioche on a wire rack.

That's it. Stand by with the butter and strawberry jam! Alternatively, wait until the brioche are cooled, cover them in clingfilm and freeze. Regenerate as for Braeval Bread (see page 180).

INDEX